THE EXPERTISE OF
THE CHANGE AGENT

THE EXPERTISE OF THE CHANGE AGENT
Public Performance and Backstage Activity

DAVID BUCHANAN
Loughborough University Business School

DAVID BODDY
University of Glasgow Business School

PRENTICE HALL
New York London Toronto Tokyo Sydney Singapore

First published in 1992 by
Prentice Hall International (UK) Ltd
Campus 400, Maylands Avenue
Hemel Hempstead
Hertfordshire HP2 7EZ
A division of
Simon & Schuster International Group

Typeset in 10/12 pt Times
by Columns Design & Production Services Ltd., Reading

Printed and bound in Great Britain by Hartnolls Limited, Bodmin

---

Library of Congress Cataloging-in-Publication Data

Buchanan, David A.
  The expertise of the change agent: public performance and
backstage activity / David Buchanan, David Boddy.
      p.   cm.
  First published 1992 by Prentice Hall International (UK) —T.p.
verso.
  Includes bibliographical references (p.   ) and index.
  ISBN 0–13–544024–6
  1. Organizational change. I. Boddy, David. II. Title.
HD58.8.B83 1992
658.4'06—dc20   91–45849
                                                           CIP

British Library Cataloguing in Publication Data

A catalogue record for this book is available from the British Library.

ISBN 0–13–544024–6

---

3   4   5   96   95   94

For Mairi

Contents

Acknowledgements

We would like to thank the many change agents who have contributed to our understanding of the topic of change management, either through direct participation in some of the research that is reported in this text, or through the discussion on management development programmes where we have addressed these issues. We wish in addition to thank our anonymous reviewer for a series of helpful criticisms and comments, and our editor at Prentice Hall, Cathy Peck, for her advice also. The errors and flaws in the text are of course fully the responsibility of the authors. We would also like to offer our sincere thanks to Carol Collier for her assistance with the presentation of the manuscript. Part of the research work mentioned in the text was carried out with the aid of a project grant from The Training Agency (now the Department of Employment Training, Education and Enterprise Division), and we wish to thank in particular Peter Reid and David Vickers for their advice and support with this project.

1

The state of the art

Is there a problem?

There are many characteristics we associate with expertise: quick, confident judgements made under pressure, a reassuring manner, and an eye for the unusual or rare variable. However, one consideration seems tantamout: that experts make better – that is, more accurate – judgements than do untrained novices. In other words, expertise should provide both superior decision processes and superior performance. (Johnson, 1988, p. 210)

The management of change is now commonly viewed as a complex and difficult area, worthy of special attention and study, from both theoretical academic and practical management viewpoints. There seem to be no easy answers, no quick fixes, and no instant solutions in this field. If there is a trend to be observed, media and academic commentary would have us believe that change is increasingly rapid and complex, and is thus becoming potentially more intractable.

What competences are required to manage organizational change effectively in the 1990s? What demands do complexity and pace make on the change agent? How can the relevant management expertise be developed? These are the central questions addressed in this book, which has the following three main aims:

1. To review recent commentary in this field.
2. To identify, from the point of view of the practitioner, the limitations of the advice derived from that commentary.
3. To introduce a fresh perspective to guide the change agent.

In pursuit of those aims we will explore four themes:

1. The nature and implications of the context of change for the role of the change agent.
2. The process of change implementation, and the shifting priorities of the change agent in managing that process.
3. The competences of the effective change agent, given the nature of the context and the process.

4.   Approaches to the development of appropriate expertise.

The argument draws initially on the experience of managing 'new' (i.e. information) technology in a variety of settings. It is now uncommon to find an organization introducing technical changes unaccompanied by other sweeping changes to manufacturing systems and administrative procedures (Peters, 1987; Preece, 1989). This focus also reflects the research and consulting experience of the authors. It will become evident, however, that the arguments and implications derived from such settings apply to organizational change in general. Experience in other settings, such as transport, aviation and major civil engineering projects, reveals a similar picture (Morris and Hough, 1987). The new technology experience merely serves as a useful source of illustrations.

This text has been designed primarily for use on postgraduate and post-experience management programmes. The text has three emphases which contrast with some other available work in this area. First, the book is primarily concerned with the change agent, and less with the content or substance of change in organizations. Second, the argument advanced here is supported by the first-hand experience of change agents drawn from the authors' research, and is not merely dependent on literature reviews and other second-hand accounts of change. Third, the text aims to identify the skills, abilities and behaviours of the effective change agent and how these can be developed, and is not solely preoccupied with theoretical development. We seek, through this approach, to develop a view of the context and process of change, and of the role of the change agent, that departs from traditional accounts. The implications of the views developed here for the practitioner are identified more explicitly in the companion title to this volume, *Take the Lead: Interpersonal skills for project managers* (Boddy and Buchanan, 1992).

Is there a problem here? The evidence suggests that, despite what is known about the effective management of change and despite the wealth of practical management literature on the subject, organizational change attempts are often bungled. The case of information technology implementation is particularly poignant. In the search for culprits for the increase in complexity and pace of change, information technology is one of the prime suspects, so it will be useful to examine that experience in some detail.

It is axiomatic that significant technical innovation generates organizational change (Boddy and Buchanan, 1986). Human performance in an information technology environment is as much a social and organizational accomplishment as a technical one. We know, from more than thirty years of research, that the application of computer technology in work organizations triggers changes in tasks and jobs, in the organization of work, in organization structures and in organizational mission or strategy (see McLoughlin and Clark, 1989, for a recent review of research).

It is not axiomatic that the organizational changes accompanying technical change will necessarily be appropriate and effective. We also know, despite the wide publicity given to the achievements of the last decade of the 'information technology revolution', that there is a high failure rate of applications and that the acceptability of some systems has been poor. We also have a well-documented understanding of the causes of implementation failures. Evidence for the claim that the main problems in this respect are organizational and managerial rather than technical is overwhelming.

Morley (1991) claims that, 'well over a quarter of the UK's major IT projects are well over budget and running late'. Miles (1990) cites a survey conducted in 1990 by the consulting firm KPMG indicating that 30 per cent of large information technology projects in Britain run over budget and over time, mainly because of the organizational problems created by the combination of scale and complexity. Hamilton (1988) cites a survey of sixty-eight companies by the IT consultancy Butler Cox, in which 46 per cent of information technology applications were delivered late, and 48 per cent were delivered over budget; part of the blame lay with organizational aspects of project management and control. The Butler Cox survey also suggests that training for project managers typically places too much emphasis on planning and control. Management skills, such as team building and communications, are more critical to project success, the report argues, and technical competence is rarely a source of problems or a cause of failure.

From a review of the North American literature, Long (1987) concluded that failures in office automation systems applications are due only 10 per cent to technical problems and 90 per cent to organizational problems such as poor planning, poor management, lack of training, and uncertainty about the problems being addressed. In recognition of this complexity, the concepts of information technology and even of computing are now more appropriately considered as multi-dimensional phenomena incorporating related aspects of hardware, software, networks, communications links, systems and procedures, and management practices. McLoughlin and Clark (1989) introduce the term 'engineering system' to express this multi-dimensionality. It is thus unrealistic in many contexts to identify technical change and organizational change as separate and distinct phenomena.

A survey of 400 British and Irish companies carried out in mid-1990 revealed that only 11 per cent had been successful in their applications of information technology, on criteria concerning breadth of applications and benefits achieved, project completion on time, and return on investment (Kearney, 1990). The report concluded that this rate 'must be judged unacceptably low', and also indicated that the reality may be bleaker since this was a self-selected set of respondents to a mail questionnaire which was presumably returned by the more competent and, in their own estimation, effective companies.

Among the recommendations for management action from this report were the following:

• Recognize that organization and people issues, not technical areas, are the barriers to success.

- Understand that organization and people issues are also the key contributors to success.
- Change the organization structure to capitalize on the strategic competitive advantages offered by IT.
- Appoint a user manager as project leader, not a computing or data processing specialist.

The main concerns here thus appear to lie with 'people issues', with organization structure, and with project leadership, and not with traditional project management and control, or issues related directly to technical developments.

Journalistic accounts consistently confirm the pessimistic picture, with potentially damaging consequences for those professionally employed in the field. One (anonymous) newspaper report from 1991 described how a large airline managed to lose £40 million in three months by running untested software, and also describes how estimates for the cost of a global computing system for a bank went from an initial £9 million to £114 million. The article offers a number of explanations for such 'horror stories'. Elegant, leading-edge systems designed in isolation may not address real business needs. Some IT departments are remote from the rest of their organizations, and have limited understanding of corporate strategies and pressures. Senior managers do not always appreciate the potential and limitations of IT. Short-term problems divert attention from long term needs.

It would seem clear from this evidence that most of the problems of effective implementation lie with organizational and managerial issues, and not directly with elements of system development and design. It would appear logical, therefore, to propose that the solutions to these problems lie primarily in the domain of project or change management.

The manager in search of practical advice concerning the problems of change implementation is apparently well served. The concerns with conceptual complexity, pace of change, and managerial intractability, have triggered a rich literature, which includes a wide range of academic studies, practical handbooks, specialized journals, and video programmes and training packages. There are also frequent conferences, seminars, workshops and training courses on change management, from a variety of providers, for change agents across a range of specialized settings, public and private sector. The implementation problems identified here are not, as we have already indicated, unique to new technology applications.

With such a wealth of advice, why should change implementation failures and problems be so evident? One explanation is that the publicity has been biased in the direction of the 'horror stories', and that success has been underrepresented. Consulting companies have a vested interest in publicizing such accounts as a basis for selling their services. The research evidence suggests, however, that the problems and concerns are widespread and genuine. A more plausible explanation is that change agents do not follow the advice on offer because of the format in which it is presented. The available literature can be accused of tending to vary between the superficially oversimplified, and the academically inaccessible. Another plausible explanation is that the advice on offer is not relevant, or is not perceived relevant to the change agent in a hurry.

In the sections that follow, we will summarize recent commentary on change management under three headings. First, we will consider the guidance offered in the project management literature, particularly with respect to IT. Second, we will examine the widely disseminated conventional wisdom which supports participative approaches to change implementation. Third, we will contrast those two approaches with sociological treatments which focus on the political, symbolic and ritualistic dimensions of organizational change. These accounts will concentrate on the main dimensions of thinking in those areas, and this will not constitute a comprehensive literature review (which would represent a project on a considerably larger scale than the one intended here). The contrasting emphases in these three approaches will enable us, at the end of this chapter, to outline the approach and arguments developed in the remainder of the book.

It is necessary to deal with three problems of definition before we proceed, concerning the concept of strategic change, the titles 'project manager' and 'change agent', and the concept of management competence. Unfortunately, it will not be possible to offer tidy and unambiguous definitions of these terms as they remain contentious, with different commentators using the terms in different ways.

Are we concerned with the management of change, or with the management of strategic change? It became fashionable in the second half of the 1980s to switch the focus of management research and commentary towards *strategic* change, and thus by implication to divert attention away from the management of changes that were more commonplace, more humdrum, operational. The literature of strategic management was seen to be strong on strategy formulation, but weak on implementation, and this switch of attention reflected this gap in understanding and practice.

In this book, we are concerned primarily with the role and activities of the change agent, irrespective of whether the change or changes in hand are strategic or not. A number of problems arise if one seeks to adopt some prior definition of strategic change. Change is strategic when the organization concerned perceives that the change is indeed strategic. That perception will then colour attitudes and behaviours with respect to the change and the change agent, independent of the prior definition of the observer. Change that is seen as strategic in one setting may well be mundane to another organization. It is also typically the case that changes that begin as or become strategic will involve the implementation of many operational or commonplace elements. On the other hand, change that begins as operational, incremental, humdrum, can become strategic through time, through wider shifts in perception and in priorities, and through linkages (sometimes predictable, sometimes surprising) with other changes (sometimes related, sometimes not) in the organization. Mintzberg (1989) points out that 'strategic' is often a useful label attached to events or changes *after* they have occurred rather than beforehand. To claim to limit one's attention to strategic changes, or indeed to changes that are not strategic, is therefore likely to be unrealistic and misleading and such a limitation is not adopted in this text.

Are we concerned with project management in particular, or with change management in general? We will use the terms 'change agent' and 'project manager' interchangeably. It is not possible always to distinguish clearly between these titles, which depend on and vary with the organizational context. Difficult to argue that the project manager is not a 'change agent'. Most consulting firms today advocate some version of 'a project management approach' to the implementation of their recommendations for organizational change. Difficult also to argue that the change agent is not a 'project manager'. Obeng (1990) argues that, to work effectively in turbulent and complex situations, project managers need to think of themselves as change agents, and act accordingly. However specific or general, and however concrete or ambiguous, the change agent is invariably concerned with one or more projects involving some combination of organizational and technological change. Our expectation is that 'conventional' (a term that we decline to define) project managers will recognize the issues raised in this book and find value in the treatment, and that 'change agents' who do not carry and who would not wish to have the title 'project manager' will similarly find this analysis of relevance to them.

The concept of management competence has become current in the early 1990s in America and Britain. This trend was initially triggered by the work of Richard Boyatzis (1982), who saw job competence in terms of underlying characteristics such as motives, traits, skills, aspects of self-image, or a body of knowledge – a wide-ranging concept, therefore. This line of reasoning has been developed in Britain through the medium of the Management Charter Initiative (MCI). The MCI has sought to establish a national scheme of management qualifications in Britain based on the systematic assessment of the competences expected at different levels of management. In this respect, the National Forum for Management Education and Development defined competence as 'the ability to perform effectively functions associated with management in a work-related situation'.

Competence is thus linked clearly with performance, and assessment is based on the assumption that areas of management can be fragmented into such component elements. For example, the MCI specification of the competences required for the award of a middle management qualification include nine units and thirty-six elements of competence, and in addition four 'personal competences' each with three or four further elements. The suggestion that management expertise and performance can be simply fragmented and thereby more effectively assessed in this manner has attracted significant criticism. Surely the activity of management is a more holistic, judgemental and creative enterprise than this? Surely it is unrealistic to specify competence independently of the context in which it is to be used? Surely the dynamic nature of management quickly renders obsolete any static identification of specific competences? The current British debate, and contrasts with American definitions and experience, are conveniently summarized in Conway and Powney (1990). The concept of management competence is more difficult to define than it might at first appear, particularly when it is to be used as the basis for a scheme of assessment and accreditation.

The work on management competences has more recently been developed in America by Quinn, Faerman, Thompson and McGrath (1990). They argue that the 'master manager' for the 1990s has eight leadership roles, each incorporating three key competences, resulting in a model of effective management performance resting on twenty-four competences. We will return briefly to their model in Chapter 5 where their approach to the development of these competences will be explained. They define competence simply as, 'the knowledge and skill necessary to perform a certain task or role' (Quinn *et al.*, 1990, p. 14). This definition appears to focus on input (knowledge and skill) rather than on output (ability to perform effectively), but this distinction may be merely semantic and have little impact in practice.

We will seek to establish in this text that the competences of the change agent are easily identified and unremarkable, and that from this perspective the job of the change agent is less complex than some analyses have sought to argue. However, we will also argue that possession of the core competences described in Chapter 4 is equivalent to possession of the right tool-kit – which does not necessarily mean that one is able to use the tools effectively to do the job. We will argue that the *expertise* of the change agent encompasses not only the tool-kit, but also the diagnostic, evaluative and judgemental capabilities required to use the tool-kit effectively. Are managerial judgement and diagnostic skills just more core competences? Not necessarily, because it is difficult to understand either competence or expertise independently of the change process, the nature of which is in turn dependent on context. The effective change agent has to be able to deploy sound understanding of context and process in order to bring the right tools to bear to achieve the desired results.

Project management models of change

The six phases of a project:
1. enthusiasm
2. disillusionment
3. panic
4. search for the guilty
5. punishment of the innocent
6. praise and rewards for the non-participants

(source unknown)

The published advice and commercial training available for project managers, as change agents, revolves around the concept of the phased project life cycle. The main emphases in this approach lie with the clear statement and definition of objectives, responsibilities, deadlines and budgets. Successful change implementation in this model is attributed to the clarity with which those dimensions are specified, and to the effectiveness of the monitoring and control which ensure that the project stays on target. Ineffective implementation in this model is attributed to the failure to specify goals, tasks, milestones and budgets clearly, and to poor project control. The project manager in this approach is thus expected to be skilled in two primary dimensions. First, with respect to the substance or content of the changes introduced (whether this is a computerized management information system, or a new factory building, or a revised payment system). Second, with respect to project control – defining outcomes and the necessary activities along the way, monitoring activity and progress, and taking remedial action to minimize deviations from the planned project life cycle. The project manager is thus expected to have 'content' and 'control' competences.

The structures of project management texts and manuals are thus typically based on a version of the project life cycle, identifying and elaborating the tools and techniques relevant to each stage. Darnell and Dale (1985), in a British Institute of Management publication concerning industrial capital investment projects, advocate a 'total approach' to project management, based on a four phase project cycle, and 'related control disciplines', involving planning, construction, commissioning, and 'run-up' (i.e. the post-commissioning stage when results are expected but when problems still remain to be solved). Paul Dinsmore (1990), in a more recent American text labels the four main phases of project development as conceptualization, planning, execution and termination. Dinsmore's (1990, p. 17) definitions of project and project management are:

> A *project* is a unique venture with a beginning and an end, conducted by people to meet established goals within parameters of cost, schedule and quality.

> *Project management* is the combination of people, systems, and techniques required to coordinate the resources needed to complete projects within established goals.

Also reinforcing the transient, goal-driven, resource-bound nature of project management, Robert Graham (for whom the four phases of a project are creation, planning, execution and ending) offers the following definition (1985, pp. 1–2):

> A project is a set of people and other resources temporarily assembled to reach a specified objective, normally with a fixed budget and with a fixed time period. Projects are generally associated with products or procedures that

are being done for the first time or with known procedures that are being altered.

In his text on 'advanced project management', the British author Fred Harrison (1985) describes the role of the project manager in terms of planning, control and 'managing people'. His text includes chapters on planning, control, cost estimating, planning tools, work breakdown techniques, performance analysis and procurement. He includes a final chapter on 'human behaviour', criticizing the lack of training for engineers in 'human relations skills' such as team building, conflict resolution, and interpersonal behaviour. Paul Dinsmore (1990) cites an American Project Management Institute definition of the 'eight areas of expertise' of project management, which include managing scope (i.e. defining boundaries), managing time, managing money, managing quality, managing communications, managing human resources, managing contracts and supply, and managing risk.

The emphasis in these accounts is consistently with planning and control. Skills in dealing with 'human factors' or 'behavioural issues' are seen as important, but tend to be another item on the list (often the last item), subordinated to the more important and much broader range of issues concerned with project planning and control tools and techniques. However, Dinsmore does argue that, from his experience, at least half of the typical problems faced by project managers are 'behavioural' rather than technical, and elaborates in his text many of the issues mentioned by Harrison, such as team building, time management, handling conflict, negotiating, communicating, decision making, and problem solving. Dinsmore's treatment is thus unusual in the emphasis given to 'human factors'; he concentrates on the interpersonal, group and structural issues and does not touch on the wider organizational and political issues covered later in this chapter and in Chapters 2 and 3.

Turning to current practice, the consulting firm PA specifies the implementation cycle for change projects (to implement the recommendations of their consulting assignments) thus:

1. Develop a strategy.
2. Confirm top level support.
3. Use a project management approach:
   (a) identify tasks;
   (b) assign responsibilities;
   (c) agree deadlines;
   (d) initiate actions;
   (e) monitor;
   (f) act on problems;
   (g) close down.
4. Communicate results.

British Telecom, in its internal project management handbook *Meeting Customer*

Requirements (1988), specifies a five-stage project approach which, in summary, includes:

Stage 1   Quality improvement proposal

Identify: clear ownership;
          crisp and clear statement of problem;
          crisp and clear statement of requirements and objectives;
          measurements;
          targets and milestones;
          plan for quality improvement team training and communication needs.

Stage 2   Problem analysis and planning

Identify: root causes;
          possible solutions;
          selected solutions;
          sub-projects;
          problem costs and benefits;
          resource requirements;
          planned action and stages;
          measurements.

Stage 3   Education and communication of action plan

Understanding and involvement of all those affected.
Identify what, why, when, where, how.

Stage 4   Detailed implementation plans

Action plans; commitment and involvement.

Stage 5   Implementation

Do; measure; assess; report.

The customers here of course are internal managers and not domestic telephone users. The British Telecom project approach is related to an eight-stage problem-solving process which follows these steps:

1. Identify problem.
2. Gather data.
3. Analyse data.
4. Generate solutions.
5. Select the solution.
6. Plan for implementation.
7. Implement and test.
8. Continue to improve.

The handbook explains: 'The 5 Stage Project Approach represents the key managerial control steps for successful improvement "breakthrough", and the Problem Solving Process the detailed "cutting wheel" that can be applied within each of the 5 stages of a project.'

With respect to computerized management information systems, Niv Ahituv and Seev Neumann (1986) portray the information system development life cycle in terms of the following ten activities:

1. Preliminary analysis.
2. Feasibility study.
3. Information analysis.
4. System design.
5. Programming.
6. Procedure development.
7. Conversion.
8. Operation and maintenance.
9. Post-audit.
10. Termination (abandonment or replacement).

These authors recommend that implementation should be the responsibility of a formally established development team reporting to a steering committee which monitors progress. They do not, however, elaborate on the skills required to manage the development life cycle or to work with the development team and steering committee.

Dealing with the same technology, Tony Gunton (1990) describes the 'conventional' system development life cycle:

> In the conventional approach to systems development, the development life-cycle is seen as a linear process divided into a number of consecutive phases. The first phase is a feasibility study or requirements analysis, designed to establish whether computer development is worthwhile and what objectives should be set for a subsequent project. This is followed successively by systems analysis, system design and programming, each of which works out the design in more detail and expresses it in terms appropriate for the computer equipment that will be used. Next follows testing and installation, and the process concludes with an enhancement and maintenance phase. (Gunton, 1990, p. 222)

Gunton argues that this linear process worked well with 'the hard and specific requirements of applications such as financial accounting and stock control', but that this is less relevant where requirements are 'soft' and in organizational environments of constant change. Increased organizational turbulence, he points out, means that changes may have to be introduced during the project life cycle, disrupting time scales and damaging the morale of the project team – with the alternative of delivering an application that no longer meets requirements. Where the context of the change is itself subject to change, Gunton argues: 'The

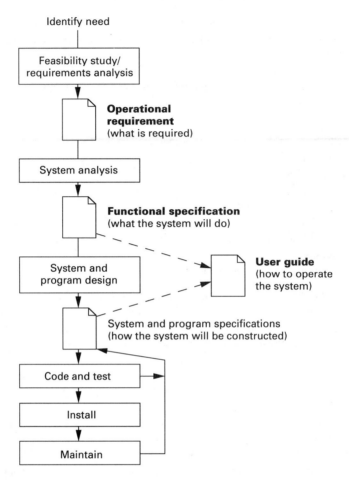

Figure 1.1   A version of the conventional system development life cycle (Source: Gunton, 1990, p. 223)

inevitable result is that too many development projects develop into a guerilla war between developers and users, with each fighting to gain territory jealously guarded by the other' (Gunton, 1990, p. 222). Gunton's portrayal of the conventional model is shown in Figure 1.1. This type of project management approach can be applied to any kind of organizational change. David Birchall (1975), for example, offers the phased model in Figure 1.2 (shown in part only for the purpose of illustration) for the step-by-step implementation of changes to job design to improve employee motivation and performance. There are many such models in the literature, and these are offered as typical illustrative examples – with common aspects. The main dimension on which these accounts vary concerns the degree of detailed elaboration of the stages of the implementation life cycle. These project management models also have two interesting features in common.

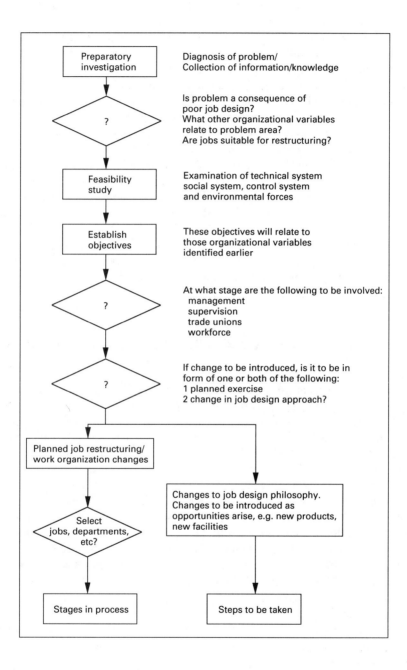

Figure 1.2 A model for job design change (Source: Birchall, 1975, p. 98)

First, they rely on the assumption that planned change in organizations unfolds in a logically sequenced manner. Solutions are not identified until the problem has been clearly defined. An effective solution is not selected until the various options have been systematically compared. Implementation does not begin until there is agreement on the solution. The key actors in the implementation process each have clearly specified tasks and responsibilities. The progress of implementation is systematically monitored and deviations from plan are corrected. The implementation process is bounded in terms both of resources (people and money) and time, with a clear termination or close-down date. The 'logical unfolding' property of these accounts has labelled them as 'rational-linear' models of change. The assumptions of rationality and linearity in organizational change have attracted significant criticism, to which we will turn later in this chapter. The logic which unfolds in this perspective is the logic of rational problem solving. This is an issue to which we will return, when contrasting this view of change management with other perspectives.

Second, they rely on the assumption that the participation or involvement of those affected by the change is but one important step in the overall implementation process. The assumption that participation is more central to effective change management is explored in the following section.

The truth, trust, love and collaboration approach to change

Ask any management group to list from their experience (positive and negative) what they would regard as the preconditions for effective change in organizations, and the terms involvement, participation, ownership, communication, commitment and trust invariably emerge. The participative approach to the management of change has become a well-established aspect of conventional wisdom. Few would now openly argue that participative management (however defined), except in extreme circumstances, is not an effective approach to the implementation of organizational change, to overcoming resistance, and to winning commitment to new ideas. Andrew Pettigrew (1985) has described this as the 'truth, trust, love and collaboration approach' to change. This is a key feature of the North American organizational development literature, and has also become an integral component of European and Scandinavian management thought and practice. The concept of establishing 'ownership' of change became central to this argument in the late 1980s. The term is generally used in a vague and imprecise manner to indicate feelings of personal involvement in and contribution to events and outcomes. The underlying, and wholly reasonable, assumption is that if people are able to say 'I helped to build this', they will be more willing to live and work with it, whatever it is.

One of the most influential studies which initiated the participative management movement was carried out by Lester Coch and John French in a pyjama factory in

Marion, Virginia – Harwood Manufacturing Corporation – in America in the 1940s. The company faced resistance from their employees to the frequent changes to jobs and work methods that developments in products and manufacturing methods forced on them. This resistance took varied forms, including complaints about pay, high absenteeism and labour turnover, poor productivity, deliberate restrictions on output, and 'marked aggression against management'. Financial incentives had proved ineffective in improving motivation and facilitating change. Coch and French (1948) were able to design an experiment with three production groups in the factory, each facing minor changes, but each given different levels of participation in introducing these changes.

In this experiment, a 'non-participation' group of eighteen hand pressers were given no say in changes to work methods, which they resisted, and which led to output restriction and hostility towards supervision. A second 'representation' group of thirteen pyjama folders were allowed to comment on proposals to change the way in which they folded jackets and trousers; this group were cooperative, efficiency ratings rose rapidly, nobody argued with supervision or the time study engineer, and nobody left the group. A third 'total participation' group of fifteen pyjama examiners were allowed to take part fully in the redesign of their inspection routine and in the calculation of new time standards. Coch and French remarked that: 'it is interesting to observe that in the meetings with these two groups suggestions were immediately made in such quantity that the stenographer had great difficulty recording them.' The total participation group increased its efficiency rating very rapidly to a level much higher than before the change, and there was no conflict.

Two and a half months after this experiment, the remaining thirteen members of the non-participation group (the others had left the company) were brought together again for a new pressing job. They followed the total participation procedure, and produced the same results as the previous total participation group – rapid rise in efficiency, no aggression, and no resignations. Coch and French thus concluded that it was not the people or personality factors, but the way in which they were treated that created or overcame resistance to the changes. Employee participation has since this study been one of the standard prescriptions for managers looking for a technique to overcome resistance and introduce change smoothly and quickly. There are countless studies in numerous journals confirming the generalizable efficacy of participative management in a wide range of organizational settings beyond pyjama manufacture.

A significant proportion of management commentary since Coch and French can be seen as attempts to offer further detailed advice on how more effectively to involve employees in the running of their organizations and in the effective implementation of change. This applies to the 'quality of working life' movement of the 1960s and 1970s (Buchanan, 1979), to the 'quality circle' movement of the 1970s and 1980s and to 'high involvement management' practices in general (Lawler, 1986). The more recent writings of Tom Peters (1987) reflect the same advice in his advocacy of self-managing teams as the basic organizational unit, and the redefined role of participative or 'facilitative' first-line supervision.

As with project management models of change implementation, the 'truth, trust, love and collaboration approach' to change lends itself to easy prescription. Goodwin Watson (1966), for example, lists twelve helpful rules for overcoming resistance to change in the 'high involvement', Coch and French style:

1. Resistance will be less if administrators, teachers, board members and community leaders feel that the project is their own – not one devised and operated by outsiders.
2. Resistance will be less if the project clearly has wholehearted support from top officials.
3. Resistance will be less if participants see the change as reducing rather than increasing their present burdens.
4. Resistance will be less if the project accords with values and ideas which have long been acknowledged by participants.
5. Resistance will be less if the programme offers the kind of new experience which interests participants.
6. Resistance will be less if participants feel that their autonomy and their security is not threatened.
7. Resistance will be less if participants have joined in the diagnostic efforts leading them to agree on what the basic problem is and to feel its importance.
8. Resistance will be less if the project is adopted by consensual group decision.
9. Resistance will be reduced if proponents are able to empathize with opponents; to recognize valid objections; and to take steps to relieve unnecessary fears.
10. Resistance will be reduced if it is recognized that innovations are likely to be misunderstood and misinterpreted, and if provision is made for feedback of perceptions of the project and for further clarification as needed.
11. Resistance will be reduced if participants experience acceptance, support, trust and confidence in their relations with one another.
12. Resistance will be reduced if the project is kept open to revision and reconsideration if experience indicates that changes would be desirable.

These look like twelve simple rules, but note the scale of management activity and time commitment implied when these neatly wrapped and generalized statements are unpacked and their detailed practical implications are worked through. The Australian management academic Dexter Dunphy (1981) argues that successful change programmes in organizations tend to have most of the following fifteen features:

1. Clear objectives.
2. Realistic scope, planned, simple.

3. Informed awareness around the organization.
4. Selection of appropriate intervention strategies.
5. Good timing.
6. Genuine participation.
7. Support from key power groups.
8. Use of existing power structure and experience.
9. Open assessment before implementation.
10. Majority support for perceived benefits.
11. Competent staff support to offer temporary resources.
12. Integration of new methods into routine operations.
13. Transfer and diffusion of successful innovations.
14. Continuing review and modification.
15. Adequate rewards for implementers and those affected.

This appears to be a straightforward blend of project management and participative management advice, with four of the fifteen items (informed awareness, genuine participation, open assessment, majority support) related directly to establishing ownership of change among those affected. However, much the same comment applies here as to Watson's twelve rules, as becomes evident when one seeks to identify the day-to-day implications of Dunphy's fifteen recommendations. This looks on the surface like easy prescription, but it is clear that, to follow this guidance and to attempt to get it right, the change management task is multi-layered, multi-faceted, and above all enormously time consuming for those leading the process.

The change agent may simply not have time, personally or even with the aid of a project team, to cover all of that ground. Similarly, the change agent and support team may not collectively possess the blend of expertise and other resources required to cover that range of issues. The role of the change agent is rarely specified with the expectation that such a range of activities should indeed be covered. And this prescription ignores the possibility that other managers are pursuing different, perhaps personal, agendas through organizational change and that the politics of the organization might lead to shifts in priorities during the life of the project.

Advice can only be regarded as realistic and practical if it is possible for the recipient to act upon it. It may well be that, in some contexts, these prescriptive accounts are wholly appropriate because the various caveats just mentioned simply do not apply. Such advice may, on the other hand, be wholly inappropriate where constraints induced by time, expertise, resources, organizational politics, job definitions, and shifting priorities prevent its application. How, then, should the change agent proceed in contexts in which this kind of advice is unrealistic and impractical? We shall attempt to provide at least a partial answer to this awkward question at the end of Chapter 3.

Still in the mode of easy prescription from a participative management perspective, Kotter and Schlesinger (1979) suggest a more parsimonious and oft-quoted list of six specific methods for change implementation to overcome resistance:

1. *Education and counselling* Management should share knowledge, perceptions and objectives with those to be affected by change. This may involve a major training programme, face-to-face counselling, group meetings, and the distribution of reports.
2. *Participation and involvement* Those who might resist should be involved in planning and implementing change. This should reduce opposition and enhance commitment. This also reduces anxieties that individuals may have about the unknown consequences of change, and also makes effective use of existing skill and knowledge.
3. *Facilitation and support* People may need to be provided with counselling and therapy to help overcome fears and anxieties about change.
4. *Negotiation and agreement* It may be necessary to establish a mutually agreeable compromise through trading and exchange. The content of change may have to be adjusted to meet the needs and interests of potential resistors.
5. *Manipulation and cooptation* This involves covert attempts to sidestep potential resistance. This can be achieved through emotional appeal to sensitive groups, and through the selective dissemination of potentially distorted information to highlight benefits and ignore disadvantages. Key resistors can be coopted by giving them privileged access to the decision-making process.
6. *Explicit and implicit coercion* Management here abandons attempts to reach consensus and resorts to the use of force or threats. This need not involve violence; it may be sufficient to offer to fire, transfer or demote individuals or to stifle their promotion and career prospects.

The last two of these techniques – manipulation and threat – are not normally prescribed as useful except in extreme circumstances. These approaches may appear to have the desired short-run effect, but can be expected to generate long-term difficulties. Manipulation when discovered can tarnish the reputations and goodwill of the perpetrators. Coopted troublemakers now have a new power base from which to make more trouble. The typical human response to threat is counter-threat, now or at some date in the future. Those subjected to what they perceive as unwarranted pressure invariably pursue more or less subtle forms of revenge. Surely such techniques cannot be considered as appropriate or ethically justifiable tools of the professional change agent? We would like to support the claim that these can be conceived as appropriate and ethical tools, if they are defined, understood and used in particular contexts.

We will argue later in this text, at the end of Chapter 3 in particular, that manipulation and threat – terms which can acquire a number of different meanings and connotations in different circumstances – must remain on the change agent's list of essential techniques. It will be suggested that the 'truth, trust, love and collaboration approach' dismisses these techniques too readily, and that in some organizational contexts these are useful and necessary methods for the implementation of change.

Kotter and Schlesinger argue that the six techniques they identify can be used in any combination, depending on circumstances, on the predicted reactions of those involved, and on the short- and long-term implications of resolving an issue in a particular way. Unilateral, directed, autocratic change management, however, is still likely to be less effective than participation in some form, they argue.

To return briefly to 'new technology', the field of systems design and of human–computer interaction is now driven by participative approaches (see, for example, Hirschheim, 1985). One well known example of participative systems design methodology is Enid Mumford's (1981; Mumford and Weir, 1979) ETHICS approach. Here the key ingredients include user involvement in system development and recognition of the social issues in implementation, including the socio-technical redesign of affected jobs. There are now a number of similar methodologies advocated for involving users in the system design process, for understanding users' needs more effectively, and for giving users wider influence in decisions concerning design parameters and operational features that will affect their work. The work of Ken Eason at Loughborough (1988; 1989) has been particularly influential in this area.

However, despite the otherwise convincing evidence in the general management literature on change concerning participative approaches, Ives and Olson (1984), from a review of twenty-two studies, conclude that the evidence to support user involvement in information system design is weak, and that the benefits of such approaches remain to be demonstrated. Child (1984) explores the circumstances in which participation may be inappropriate or unworkable. While supporting the view that the involvement of those to be affected by change is ethically desirable, Child argues that where there is full agreement on how to proceed, or where management is powerful enough to force changes through, participation may be seen simply as a waste of time. Similarly, where there is fundamental disagreement and inflexible opposition to change, participation may be used to obstruct implementation. Child also cites American research suggesting that it is wholly unrealistic to think of moving to consensus through participation in large public sector bureaucracies with rigid hierarchies pervaded by competing political interest groups. Some large private sector companies have these bureaucratic and political characteristics too.

Sustaining belief in the power of participative approaches, and contradicting that last finding, a report by Ingersoll Engineers (1987) concerning applications of advanced manufacturing technology claims that, 'our research reveals that there are really only three fundamental criteria for success', which are:

1. that technology should be part of an overall plan or strategy to serve business needs;
2. that the attempted leap in technology must not be too great; and
3. that the people concerned must be closely involved.

The report continues:

> The biggest single barrier to success is the failure to involve people.
> Wherever we've seen manufacturing technology achieve its full capability,
> the people on the shop floor feel a measure of ownership in it, and union
> officials feel deeply involved too. In every case of failure we've seen, these
> non-manufacturing people issues were not tackled vigorously enough.
> (Ingersoll Engineers, 1987, p. x)

It should not be surprising that half a century of management commentary has
consistently sustained the belief in the efficacy of participative methods. The
notion that people should be involved in changes which affect their lives is
consistent with Western democratic value systems – political, religious and social.
The notion that people will be more comfortable with and more committed to
changes that they have decided for themselves, and not had forced upon them, is
also consistent with Western notions of freedom, individualism, and the proactivity
of human nature.

The model of the effective change agent that emerges from these accounts
incorporates sensitivity to the needs and interests of a range of stakeholders in the
organization and even beyond who may be affected in a range of positive and
negative ways by a particular programme of change. The competences of the
change agent in this domain concern interpersonal and social skills such as
communication, listening, building effective relationships and team building. In
contrast with the 'content' and 'control' skills emphasized by the project
management literature, here the concern is more with what can be described as
'process' skills. We noted following our discussion of the project management
literature of change that the dominant unfolding logic is the logic of problem
solving. The dominant unfolding logic in the participative management view of
change is the logic of establishing ownership in those directly affected.

The politics of change

Define the goals and the process of change clearly, monitor and control the process
carefully, and involve those who are going to be affected, avoiding where possible
the use of manipulation and threat. These would seem to be the main messages
from the project and participative management literatures briefly reviewed so far.
Stated in this manner, it is difficult to see where one could establish points of
disagreement with such prescription. The absence of clearly defined goals and
responsibilities, the absence of adequate control, the absence of meaningful
involvement, and the autocratic imposition of change through manipulation, threat
and direct command, would all thus appear to be the ingredients of failure and
disaster.

Were the implementation of organizational change as straightforward as that advice implies, there would perhaps be fewer accounts of failed and unsuccessful change in circulation. It is therefore not surprising to find that numerous commentators have indicated other dimensions of organizational change which render the process less rational, non-linear, and more complex, and which in turn render simplistic the management advice we have examined so far.

The 'rational-linear' model of change as a logically unfolding sequence has attracted significant criticism. Richard Whipp *et al.* (1988, p. 51) criticize what has elsewhere been described as 'the commander model' of change implementation (Bourgeois and Brodwin, 1984). This model can be regarded as an extreme and idealized interpretation of the project management approach described earlier, with change driven by omnipotent managers with known and consistent preferences, and with adequate information and clear organization. The commander model also assumes rational analysis of environment and resources, the systematic revelation and assessment of alternatives, followed by implementation of the logical choice of solution. Whipp *et al.* argue that change is more likely to involve a number of actors, representing different levels and sections of the organization, pulling in different directions, in the pursuit of personal as well as organizational goals:

Strategic processes of change are now more widely accepted as multi-level activities and not just as the province of a few, or even a single, general manager. Outcomes of decisions are no longer assumed to be a product of rational or boundedly rational debates, but are also shaped by the interests and commitments of individuals and groups, forces of bureaucratic momentum, and the manipulation of the structural context around decisions and changes. (Whipp *et al.*, 1989, p. 51)

What becomes recognized as 'strategy', therefore, can often be a reconstruction after the fact (a point noted earlier in this chapter). Strategy in this perspective is 'emergent' in that it can be seen to be derived from a series of smaller-scale and incremental changes, rather than the conventional view of strategy as a rationally intended grand master plan set out in advance. This view of organizational change as 'logical incrementalism' was originally identified by Quinn (1980) who saw the development of strategy as both a political and an analytical process characterized by 'muddling through with purpose'. Change is thus seen as a cumulative process, in which the 'strategic' is an accretion of smaller steps, and in which the process is an evolutionary one of trial, error, experimentation and learning, rather than one of early commitment to a radical longer-term fixed plan. We will return to Quinn's account in Chapter 3.

There have been a number of sociologically inspired analyses of change implementation which criticize both the lack of attention to the process and context of change, and the rational-linear view of that process. These analyses emphasise the political and cultural nature of the change process (Quinn, 1980; Pettigrew, 1985 and 1987) and seek to demonstrate how the rational and political dimensions are intertwined. Five commentators (among others) who address practical aspects of the task of the project manager or change agent working with systemic, strategic technical and organizational change, are Markus (1983), Robey and Lynne (1988), Pettigrew (1985; 1987), Kanter (1983) and Johnson (1990).

M. Lynne Markus (1983), for example, identifies the following four broad types of resistance to change:

1. *People-focused* Here the blame lies with the individuals, their personalities, their attitudes, values, preferences, or perhaps age.
2. *System-focused* Here the problem lies with system designers and with equipment characteristics such as 'user-friendliness', complexity, ergonomic features, access for maintenance and so on.
3. *Organization-focused* Here the cause of resistance lies with the perceived lack of fit between the system and its organizational context. The key factor here concerns the allocation of responsibilities. Technological and procedural changes often mean new patterns of working and changes to social relationships in the organization. This can cut across traditional cultures and established ways of doing things, and can affect real and presumed status differentials.
4. *Politics-focused* Here the explanation for resistance lies with the interaction between system and context. But the key factor this time is distribution of power. New procedures and technologies alter the ownership of information, alter patterns of access to information, and affect established patterns of decision making and the exercise of influence by individuals and groups.

While resistance to change can be caused by any of these factors, and any combination, Markus argues that organization-focused and politics-focused explanations are more common, and examines the circumstances in which this is likely to be the case, particularly with respect to what she labels as the political variant:

> the political variant is most appropriate when conditions likely to produce political decision-making obtain; when there is disagreement about organizational goals and values; when uncertainty exists about the means required to produce the desired objectives; when resources are scarce; when the decisions are important.

> the political variant is the most appropriate analytical framework when organizational participants disagree about the nature of the problem that a system is proposed to solve, when there exists uncertainty about whether a particular proposed system will solve the problem, and when the power bases allocated are highly valued and in short supply. These conditions are most likely to be met when the information system cuts horizontally across several diverse organizational sub-units and has many different types of users. (Markus, 1983, p. 443)

This approach has more than theoretical interest in framing appropriate explanations for resistance. Interesting practical implications flow from this analysis. If the causes of resistance are person- or system-based, then the solutions can be relatively easy to identify and implement; better training, better staff, better design, better designers. However, if the causes are in the organizational and political domains, solutions are not as clear-cut and obvious, and the appropriate action may be considerably more complex and time consuming as well as more difficult to establish to begin with.

Robey and Lynne (1988) argue that systems designers and managers need to be aware of the importance of ritual in change implementation in organizations. This account contrasts the rational and political perspectives on systems design and implementation arguing that the presence of competing motives and opportunities in the community of actors engaged in change render the process a political one. While highlighting the role of political activity and ritual in the process of change, and advocating management sensitivity to these issues, Robey and Lynne do not address in any depth the practical skills implications of their argument that 'it is essential for those engaged in the process to be aware of what is really going on' (p. 207).

What is the significance of ritual in organizational change? Ritual refers here simply to regular processes and events in the organization that have specific purposes and which thus carry specific meanings within the culture of the organization and for its members. The annual conference, the Director's report, the quarterly review, capital investment appraisal procedures, the Christmas party, the monthly staff meeting, department audits ... are all potential examples of organizational rituals, which have different meanings and serve different purposes for different organizations. With respect to new technology applications in particular, Robey and Lynne explain this in the following terms:

> Rituals in systems development function to maintain the appearance of rationality in systems development and in organizational decision making. Regardless of whether it actually produces rational outcomes or not, systems development must symbolize rationality and signify that the actions taken are not arbitrary, but rather acceptable within the organization's ideology. As such, rituals help provide meaning to the actions taken within an organization. By performing this function, systems design rituals uphold the myth, central to Western society, that organizations are rational entities serving social interests by pursuing their own goals. Myths are not necessarily false; their essential characteristic is that they are widely believed. Since a lore of rationality surrounds both computing and organizational decision making, it is completely understandable that the systems development process be regarded as rational also. The rituals help to ensure this perception. (Robey and Lynne, 1988, pp. 206–7)

Ritual in this context thus concerns action by the change agent which serves to 'maintain the appearance of rationality' and which is 'acceptable within the organization's ideology'. Before dismissing rational-linear models of change, it is necessary to consider the symbolic function of such processes in sustaining the 'myth of organizational rationality' and, by implication, sustaining the legitimacy of the change agent. Such linear models may have a poor relationship with the actual unfolding of organizational changes, while in practice playing a significant symbolic and legitimating function in scripting the ritual that the change agent is both required and expected to follow to gain organizational acceptance.

Pettigrew (1985) advocates a perspective on strategic change implementation that recognizes the combination of rational, cultural and political factors in decision making, and that also takes into account the influence of historical and contextual factors in relation to the continuous process of change. This perspective again takes issue with rational-linear models of change which are dismissed as inadequate ways of theorizing events and as oversimplified guides to appropriate management action. The managerial process in Pettigrew's view is a complex and untidy cocktail of ostensibly rational assessment mixed with differential perceptions, quests for power, visionary leadership, and the 'subtle processes' of marshalling support for ideas.

Pettigrew has been concerned with the management of strategic change, which is defined in the following way:

> strategic changes are viewed as streams of activity involving at various times the differential attention of individuals and groups, which occur mainly but not solely as a consequence of environmental change, and which can lead to alterations in the product market focus, structure, technology, and culture of the host organization. Strategic is just a description of magnitude of change in, for example, structure and organizational culture, recognizing the second-order effects, or multiple consequences of any such changes. (Pettigrew, 1985, p. 438)

We are thus here concerned with change on a scale and of a scope beyond the manner in which pyjamas are folded.

Central to Pettigrew's analysis of 'the processual dynamics of changing' is a concern with the 'management of meaning' and with the processes through which change – which may be strategic or may concern garment folding methods – is legitimized. This analysis is a clear challenge to the 'truth, trust, love and collaboration approach to change', and clearly has concerns in common with those raised by Robey and Lynne. And in addition to the concerns raised earlier with respect to the content, control and process agendas of the change agent, Pettigrew highlights the influential and potentially legitimating role of the context into which change is introduced.

Turning to the practical implications of this view, Pettigrew highlights the need for skills in intervening in an organization's political and cultural systems. These skills include building adequate support for proposals, and the simultaneous management of the content, context and process of change and the relationships between these three sets of factors. Pettigrew offers little detail on what these 'intervention skills' and 'simultaneous management' processes mean in practice. He also distinguishes between inner and outer context. The inner context of change relates to the history of the organization, its structure, its culture and its political system. The outer context of change relates to environmental factors, such as competitor behaviour, or customer demands, the sources 'from which much of the legitimacy for change is derived' (Pettigrew, 1987, p. 650). We will return to Pettigrew's view of the change agent in action in Chapter 3.

Kanter (1983) argues that the change agent in the modern corporation requires a portfolio of 'power skills' to overcome resistance and apathy to new ideas. She identifies a number of manipulative techniques for blocking interference from those who would impede change, similar to those indicated by Pettigrew. We shall return to this perspective also in Chapter 3. Kanter argues that power skills, team skills and 'change architect' skills are required to hold together what she describes as a three-stage change process involving problem definition, coalition building, and mobilization and completion respectively.

Continuing with the theme of intervention in an organization's political systems, Johnson (1990) contrasts traditional rational planning models of change with management action in what he calls the 'cognitive, cultural and political context' of the organization. He argues, consistent with the view of Robey and Lynne, that the mechanisms of change are both substantive and symbolic. Organizational symbols in this respect can be any objects, acts, or events that serve as vehicles for conveying meaning. Johnson argues that:

> It would be naive to conceptualize the manager as reconstructing anew the way in which every new problem or opportunity is to be dealt with. Rather managers become familiar with, and will learn to lean on, the routines that have evolved in the organization, routines which themselves may come to take on the role of organizational myths and rituals. (Johnson, 1990, p. 186)

The routines of project proposals and task force presentations and senior management briefings can thus be seen as 'ceremonial acts'. One of the (many) paradoxes of change, in this view, thus concerns the change agent's use of familiar, traditional and acceptable organizational procedures to promote the dismantling of other organizational arrangements and the introduction of the new.

Change is as much concerned with changing the world view or the organizational view of those involved, as it is with changing decision-making processes, payment systems, technologies or organization structures. This means challenging, questioning and breaking down the existing shared assumptions, or 'interpretive schemes', or 'cognitive coping mechanisms', held by the organization's members, in order to change attitudes and behaviour. This also means building and signalling a 'counter-culture' with a new 'dominant logic' (Johnson, 1990, p. 187). Johnson notes that it is not clear how and why symbolic action plays this challenging and reconstructing role. Such action may incorporate the visionary articulations of charismatic leaders, and their exemplary acts and statements. Other specific symbolic acts in Johnson's view include:

Symbolic acts	*Examples in practice*
Unfreezing	Challenge existing arrangements, close down sections of the organization, move people.
Flux	Foster conflict and dissent through open argument.
Information building	Hire consultants, set up task forces, commission special reports.
Experimentation	Signal change activity through management development programmes, the display of new products and services, and other new departures.
Refreezing	Send signals of irreversible and permanent change, through celebrations or new key appointments.

These symbolic acts serve both to legitimize the behaviour of the change agent, and to manipulate the views of other organizational members of the 'unfolding logic' of change, what it means, and what it entails. It is through such action, for example, that Pettigrew's 'management of meaning' is achieved. Johnson also argues that, while such actions are familiar to most managers and as such are recognized readily in the context of management training programmes, they rarely find systematic treatment in prescriptive management texts.

The model of the effective change agent that emerges from these accounts concerns sensitivity to the power and influence of key individuals and groups in the organization, including the change agent(s), and to how patterns of power and influence will be altered by a particular programme of change. The competences of the change agent here concern negotiating and selling (of plans and ideas), manipulating perceptions of the context and how it legitimizes change proposals, and the use of accepted organizational rituals further to legitimize change and the actions of the change agent. These competences include the interpersonal and social skills of communication, listening, building effective relationships and team building mentioned earlier – but here deployed with a view more towards building credibility, marshalling support and blocking interference than with understanding and dealing directly with the needs and anxieties of those affected by the changes. These competences include also the ability to engage in symbolic action which will trigger and signify and reinforce changes in shared assumptions about the organization, its purpose, and its modes of operation. These issues represent a concern with 'process' skills, but clearly relate to more than the processes of communication, involvement and participation.

We noted earlier that in the project management literature the dominant unfolding logic is the logic of problem solving. The dominant unfolding logic in the participative management view of change is the logic of establishing ownership in those directly affected. The dominant unfolding logic in the political variant as described here is the logic of establishing legitimacy.

The argument: performing and backstaging

How does the change agent, faced with complexity and pace in the turbulent context of the modern organization, handle the demands of the content, control and process agendas?

The central argument of this book is that the change agent has to support the 'public performance' of rationally considered and logically phased and visibly participative change with 'backstage activity' in the recruitment and maintenance of support and in seeking and blocking resistance. The public performance typically follows the ritual and legitimating script of the rational-linear model of project management. 'Backstaging' is concerned with the exercise of 'power skills', with 'intervening in political and cultural systems', with influencing, negotiating and selling, and with 'managing meaning'. This is achieved in a *creative* way, through appropriate symbolic actions in attempts to legitimize change by suggesting different and new interpretations of events inside and outside the organization.

The prescriptions of commentators who emphasize the political and cultural dimensions of change are thus inconsistent with conventional treatments in which manipulation, coercion, threat and symbolic action are not identified as useful components of the project manager's tool-kit. The symbolic use of ritual, the management of meaning, and the exercise of power skills do not commonly feature in project management training programmes and manuals. The project manager in search of practical advice could find confusion in these contrasting views from the literature. One reason for these contrasts, and perhaps for any ultimate confusion, may lie in the different logics emphasized by the three different approaches we have described here. Project management relies on the logic of problem solving, emphasizing the phasing of diagnosis, identification of solutions, and implementation. Participative management relies on the logic of ownership, emphasizing the role of communication, of participation, and of commitment. The political variant relies on the logic of legitimacy, emphasizing the processes of selling and convincing, team building, and blocking resistance. The expertise of the change agent thus lies in managing the parallel unfolding of these logics in a manner appropriate in the organizational context. Problems have to be seen to be solved in a suitable fashion. Those affected have to be seen to be involved in the process. The change and the change agent have to be seen to be credible and legitimate.

The argument of this book, which is developed through perspectives of the context and process of change and of the role of the change agent, relies on five main propositions.

First, the change agent in any setting has to address three parallel agendas. These are as follows:

1. *The content agenda* The project manager is expected to be technically competent and experienced with respect to the substance of the changes being implemented – for example, with respect to the hardware and software capabilities and limitations of a networked management information system.
2. *The control agenda* The project manager is expected to be familiar and competent with a range of planning, scheduling, budgeting, resourcing and monitoring techniques, with setting and meeting deadlines and targets – the staple fare of project management courses.
3. *The process agenda* Sometimes covered under the heading of implementation skills, the project manager is expected to be competent in communications and consultation, in team building, in influencing and negotiating skills, and in the management of enthusiasm and resistance.

The project management literature concentrates on content and control agendas. The participative management literature focuses on the social and interpersonal skills aspects of the process agenda. The sociological literature concentrates on the political, symbolic and ritual dimensions of the process agenda and on aspects of context.

Second, the context in which the change agent operates varies from setting to setting on a number of dimensions, but particularly with respect to the personal vulnerability to which the change agent is exposed. Analysis of accounts by change agents of their actions suggests that the context of change is experienced in terms of four main components. These concern the ways in which goals and priorities change through time, organizational interdependencies, responsibility for change and its outcomes, and the postures adopted by top management. These four dimensions are labelled, for reference, as:

1. shifting sands;
2. interlocking;
3. ownership; and
4. senior stance.

It is the nature of these four dimensions that determine the vulnerability of the change agent, and which thus shape the experience and role of the change agent in that context. The vulnerability of the change agent is likely to be high where goals and priorities change frequently, where there are many complex organizational interdependencies, where change responsibilities are ambiguous, and where senior management is either hostile or indifferent with respect to the changes in hand. Vulnerability is likely to be low where goals and priorities are stable, where organizational interdependencies are few and simple, where responsibilities are clear, and where top management is concerned and supportive.

Third, the agenda priorities of the change agent depend on context, with the content and control agendas being most significant in a low vulnerability context, and the process and control agendas taking priority in a high vulnerability context. Context factors and agenda priorities thus shape the nature of the task and of the demands placed on the change agent. It is suggested that change agents who combine a limited technical background with strong process skills can be very effective in high vulnerability contexts, whereas change agents with sound technical understanding and limited process skills are more likely to excel in low vulnerability contexts.

Fourth, the management competences relevant to the process agenda are unremarkable and relatively well understood. They are identified here in five clusters concerning, respectively, goal specification, role specification, communication, negotiation, and managing up. However, these competences can in fact be seen as a blend of skills and personality traits, raising questions concerning appropriate models of management development and behaviour change in this field. We will argue that the possession of these competences alone is necessary but not sufficient, and that the broader concept of *expertise* is required, incorporating the diagnostic, evaluative and judgemental capabilities that lead to the effective and creative use of the tool-kit of core competences to achieve the desired results in a given context. However, expertise is not merely to be understood as the effective use of a list of competences or tools. Expertise in the view developed here is concerned instead with the deployment of these competences in managing the three parallel unfolding logics of problem solving, ownership and legitimation – logics which will assume different relative priorities in different organizational and change process contexts.

Finally, the change agent in a high vulnerability context is advised in the perspective developed here to proceed in a manner that represents the rational-linear model of change, while supporting that approach with significant 'behind the scenes' action. The rational-linear model of change which dominates the project management literature and which has attracted significant criticism from sociological analyses, is thus a model for what the change agent has to be seen to do, and is only in part a model of what the change agent must actually do. The consistent semblance of a rational-linear approach to the management of change, it is argued, is vital to the perceived credibility of the change agent and to the perceived legitimacy of the changes being considered.

The argument of the book as a whole is summarized in Figure 1.3, and this is elaborated in Chapter 5.

Viewed from this angle, the criticism of rational-linear models of change in the sociological literature is misplaced in omitting to emphasize the legitimating role of those models in organizational practice. The logic of problem solving must be seen, in most organizations, to unfold in the expected and acceptable manner. However, this public performance has to be supported by *backstaging* – the politicking, the wheeler-dealing, the fixing and negotiating, the coalition building and the trade-offs – which typically cannot be openly discussed in the organization without damaging individual credibility or the legitimacy of the change attempt. The significance of the backstage activity in supporting and sustaining the public

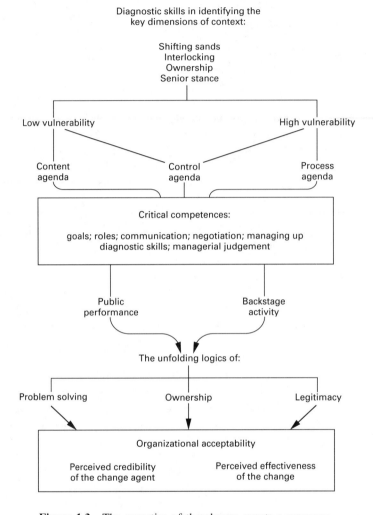

Figure 1.3   The expertise of the change agent: a summary

performance of the change agent is particularly acute in high vulnerability contexts. In this context, the logics of ownership and legitimacy must also unfold in their own time and in their own respective ways. This view is consistent with accounts of the management of change as 'the management of meaning' where emphasis is placed on the symbolic actions of the change agent – aspects of the role which are rarely expressed in the traditional project management field.

An attempt is thus made to synthesize rational-linear and political accounts of organizational change by suggesting that these are interdependent components of a process in which the establishment and maintenance of credibility and legitimacy are central to the perceived effectiveness of the change agent, and ultimately to the perceived success of change. Given that relative importance and priorities will depend on context, the change agent generally has to ensure that the three logics identified here unfold in ways that are perceived to be appropriate and acceptable in that context.

Chapter 2 concerns the context of change, the widely discussed development of 'organic' organizational forms (also described as 'adhocracy' and as 'integrative' and 'fuzzy' structures), and presents data from an analysis of eight personal accounts of organizational change to reveal four dimensions of context of significance to the change agent. The argument is supported with further data from a national survey.

Chapter 3 explores models of the process of change concentrating on political and cultural dimensions. It is argued here that competence cannot be understood or expressed independently of the process of change. One of the main recurring themes in the models explored in this chapter concerns the extent to which the change agent is required to resort to manipulative and devious behaviour, and it is argued that techniques of manipulation and threat be added to the tool-kit of the change agent.

Chapter 4 identifies five competence clusters and fifteen specific competences of the change agent. The unremarkable nature of these is noted, and their relationship with the process model established in Chapter 3 is discussed. The argument here is again supported by data from personal accounts of change and by survey data.

Chapter 5 begins by summarizing some of the recent literature from cognitive psychology on the nature of expertise, and relates this to the work of the organizational change agent. Although psychology research has concerned radically different types of task and activity, the findings of that work with respect to the nature and development of expertise are broadly consistent with our argument concerning change management expertise. The model of the effective change agent developed in the previous chapters is then summarized, and the chapter indicates how such expertise can be developed, through a flexible action-learning programme. The future research agenda, with respect to both change management and also to the appropriate development of change management expertise, is addressed.

2

Managing in quadrant four

The organic, fluid, adaptive organization

Fuzzy and crisp structures

In general terms, we define structure as providing a relatively enduring set of rules for decision making. For the moment, the degree of fuzziness (or conversely the degree of crispness) is a convenient summarizing variable for structure and the nature of these rules; some rules are elastic and fuzzy, others are tight and crisp.

We can see fuzzy structures as closely related to the notion of organic organizations and crisp structures related to mechanistic organizations as outlined by Burns and Stalker (1961). As in their theory, we posit that the fuzzy structure is suitable for coping with conditions of high uncertainty whereas crisp structures are for coping with conditions of low uncertainty. (Butler, 1991, p. 15)

Some commentators have pointed to the trend for middle management roles to become more change- and project-oriented (Kanter, 1989; Dopson and Stewart, 1990). Tom Peters (1987, p. 369) claims that the middle management function is becoming a combination of 'expeditor/barrier-destroyer/facilitator', 'on-call expert', and 'diffuser of good news', particularly with respect to the management of change. Sue Coutts (1989) offers journalistic evidence for the shift to project-based management particularly in publishing, broadcasting, journalism and the general entertainments industry; she profiles the events director for the 1988 Glasgow Garden Festival as an example of a typical short-term contract project manager. Organizational change from these accounts appears to be increasingly untidy and 'programmatic', characterized by the evolutionary unfolding of interrelated, overlapping and loosely bounded projects with shifting goals, shifting priorities, and with shifting team membership. This characterization of project-based management contrasts sharply with the accounts and definitions of project management introduced in Chapter 1.

The change agent in such contexts is thus working with considerable uncertainty, often operating outwith the conventional command and control structures of traditional organization hierarchies. For example, multi-disciplinary project teams even in smaller companies often draw together managers and professional staff, with quite different backgrounds, over whom the project leader has no clear or direct management authority. This situation is common in the construction industry, where project managers frequently find themselves working with and through subcontractors and their agents, seeking to establish coordination and cooperation without the authority to command and control directly.

Such contexts have been identified in the organization theory literature as 'fuzzy' and as 'organic', and we will explore this phenomenon in more depth shortly. Directive management as a source of access to resources and commitment in such circumstances has to be replaced by the discrete and tactful exercise of influencing and negotiating skills.

It is a straightforward observation that the organizational context will shape and influence the pressures and demands placed on the change agent and hence the nature of the task. In this chapter, we will explore attempts to understand and to conceptualize that context – the shift from bureaucracy to 'adhocracy' is one way of expressing this – and report research which sought to establish how the organizational context of change is experienced by the change agent. In this latter respect, we will be concerned with what has been called the 'phenomenological texture' of the experience – that is, how context presents itself to and is understood by the practising change agent, relying on first-hand, personal accounts.

It has long been argued that the nature of the environment or 'outer context' of an organization influences the most appropriate form of structuring or internal context. However dated, the contemporary significance of this argument is potentially sustained by the perception that, for most organizations, the external environment has become, and is increasingly, uncertain, changing, unpredictable and turbulent. The classic formulation of this case is that by Tom Burns and George Stalker (1961). They distinguish two ideal types of management system. Mechanistic management systems, with characteristics similar to bureaucracy, are appropriate and effective in dealing with stable environments. Organic systems, in contrast, are required if an organization is to deal effectively with environmental turbulence. This distinction is summarized in Table 2.1.

Mechanistic management systems use fixed job descriptions, clear management hierarchies with explicit lines of responsibility and authority, and rely on position power when decisions have to be taken (that is, the person with the superior position in the hierarchy decides). Organic management systems, in contrast, rely on loose and flexible job descriptions, have vaguely defined lines of authority and responsibility, and depend on expert power to take decisions, regardless of where in the organization the expertise happens to reside.

Burns and Stalker argue that the relative effectiveness of these two ideal types of management system depends on environmental characteristics, and that neither is necessarily correct. Note that Burns and Stalker were arguing in 1961 that organizations had a notional choice of management system, depending on the

Table 2.1 Mechanistic and organic management systems

Feature	Mechanistic	Organic
Job definitions	rigid, many	fluid, few
Standardization	specified methods	individual discretion
Conflict resolution	by the boss	by interaction
Authority	hierarchical	dispersed
Decision making	position power	expertise
Communications	proper channels	as required
Loyalty	to the organization	to the group
Status	based on position	based on contribution

nature of their product markets and technology. This is a choice between the routinization of activity on the one hand and the wider mobilization of expertise and opening of communications on the other. The choice is notional, because the management of an organization facing extremely turbulent environmental conditions could decide to soldier on with their preferred and traditional mechanistic management system – and presumably either be less successful in their enterprise, or fail.

Burns and Stalker also noted that some of us find the fluidity and ambiguity of organic structures uncomfortable, in contrast with the certainty of role and status in bureaucratic, mechanistic organizations. There is security to be found in the clearly defined job title and predictable career ladder, features which organic structures avoid. In contrast, organic structures allow individuals considerably more freedom to manoeuvre in the absence of clearly delineated job boundaries, responsibilities and lines of command. The role of the change agent in an organic environment, in terms of the pressures, demands, constraints and opportunities, is thus likely to be quite different from that in a mechanistic environment, requiring different skills and behaviours. It is interesting to note that in the context of part of our discussion in Chapter 4 tolerance of ambiguity can be a critical variable here.

The contingent structure argument of Burns and Stalker was expressed in interestingly different terms by Fred Emery and Eric Trist (1965) who offer the following typology of organizational environments:

Type 1. Placid, randomized

This is a simple, stable environment. Although external events may be unpredictable, the organization can function independently, as a single separate unit, as in the pure competition of the economic model.

Type 2. Placid, clustered

This is a slowly changing environment in which the organization survives through accurate prediction of events. Planning is thus important. Organizations become larger and hierarchical to meet this need.

Type 3. Disturbed, reactive

Here there are a number of similar organizations that the focal organization must consider. Predictive ability is confounded by these competitors, and this context is similar to oligopoly. Organizational survival is dependent partly on flexibility, which encourages decentralization.

Type 4. Turbulent field

The organization here faces a highly complex and rapidly changing environment, driven by three forces. First, the increasing interconnectedness of organizations themselves. Second, the interdependences between organizations and the societies in which they are located. Third, the competitive necessity of research and development. The end result is greatly increased uncertainty.

Following Burns and Stalker, Emery and Trist argue that the successful organizations in Type 1 environments are likely to be mechanistic, with bureaucratic structures, and standardized working procedures, dealing with little uncertainty and few changes. The successful organizations in Type 4 environments, on the other hand, have decentralized organic structures that enable them to deal effectively with high uncertainty and considerable change.

This contingency approach to organization structures and management systems implies variation in environmental characteristics between the extremes of stability and turbulence. Writing less than ten years after Burns and Stalker, Warren Bennis implies that most organizations may no longer face that extreme variance: most organizations now face turbulent environments, and Bennis predicts the death of mechanistic, bureaucratic structures as a result:

> The social structure of organizations of the future will have some unique characteristics. The byword will be 'temporary'. There will be adaptive, rapidly changing temporary systems. These will be task forces organized around problems to be solved by groups of relative strangers with diverse professional skills. The group will be arranged on an organic rather than mechanical model; it will evolve in response to a problem rather than to programmed role expectations. The executive thus becomes coordinator or 'linking pin' between various task forces. People will be evaluated not according to rank but according to skill and professional training ....
>
> Adaptive, problem-solving, temporary systems of diverse specialists, linked together by coordinating and task evaluating executive specialists in an organic flux – this is the organizational form that will gradually replace bureaucracy as we know it. As no catchy phrase comes to mind, I call these new style organizations adaptive structures. (Bennis, 1969, p. 34)

Alvin Toffler (1970) was able to think of a catchy phrase; he speaks of the decline of bureaucracy and the development of 'adhocracy' as an alternative organizational form, driven by change and by the increasing need for organizational flexibility and responsiveness to market trends.

The argument that external change promotes the development of organic, fluid, adaptive internal structures has, like participative management, persisted. Rosabeth Moss Kanter, echoing Burns and Stalker, distinguishes between 'segmentalist' (mechanistic) and 'integrative' (organic) management structures:

> I found that the entrepreneurial spirit producing innovation is associated with a particular way of approaching problems that I call 'integrative': the willingness to move beyond received wisdom, to combine ideas from unconnected sources, to embrace change as an opportunity to test limits. To see problems integratively is to see them as wholes, related to larger wholes, and thus challenging established practices – rather than walling off a piece of experience and preventing it from being touched or affected by any new experiences . . . .
>
> Such organizations reduce rancourous conflict and isolation between organizational units; create mechanisms for exchange of information and new ideas across organizational boundaries; ensure that multiple perspectives will be taken into account in decisions; and provide coherence and direction to the whole organization. In these team-oriented cooperative environments, innovation flourishes . . . .
>
> The contrasting style of thought is anti-change-oriented and prevents innovation. I call it 'segmentalism' because it is concerned with compartmentalizing actions, events, and problems and keeping each piece isolated from the others . . . . Companies where segmentalist approaches dominate find it difficult to innovate or to handle change. (Kanter, 1983, pp. 27–8)

The specific emphases in Kanter's account are thus with the eradication of organizational boundaries, and with creative thinking and problem solving. The parallels between the mechanistic–organic and the segmentalist–integrative distinctions are, however, clear. This distinction is mirrored also in the identification of fuzzy and crisp structures, in the quote from Richard Butler (1991, p. 15) which opened this chapter.

Pettigrew (1987) distinguishes between inner and outer context in relation to change. The inner context of change relates to the history of the organization, its structure, its culture and its political system. The outer context of change includes environmental factors, such as competitor behaviour, or customer requests, or technological innovations. Pettigrew (1987, p. 650) argues that the outer context offers the sources 'from which much of the legitimacy for change is derived'. The manager who can point to events outside the organization as the basis for proposing internal change stands a better chance of obtaining ready support than the manager who is perceived to be championing change for personal gain. This becomes a ready source of change legitimation as the outer context itself becomes more turbulent and crisis prone.

Is there any support for the claim that the contemporary organizational context has indeed become typically more organic, fluid and adaptive? Most managers would respond positively to this question, and be able support that intuition with personal experience. The evidence on this issue is, unfortunately, incomplete and inconclusive. There is much commentary supporting this view, but little hard data. It seems clear that this trend, broadly specified, has affected some organizations in more or less the predicted directions, but there is no evidence to indicate how widespread this trend might be, or how reliable the predictions might be in detail. Three sets of data, from Ashridge Management Centre, Templeton College Oxford, and the British Institute of Management, offer broadly consistent and confirmatory results.

A research report conducted by Ashridge Management Centre, based on a study of ten leading European companies, offers some support for the claim that organization structures are tending to become more organic and adaptable (Ashridge Management Research, 1988; Devine, 1988). This study asked what the sample companies 'are doing to stay successful in the global markets of the 1990s'. One common concern in the companies covered in this study was 'how to equip managers to function in a more complex international environment'. Changes in organization structure, the research revealed, had led to decentralization of decision making and to flatter hierarchies, and had increased the ambiguity facing managers. Internationalization had also tended to obscure organizational boundaries. The report argues for the development of the 'flexible manager', which involves:

- awareness of and ability to relate to the economic, social and political environment;
- ability to manage in a turbulent environment;
- ability to manage with complex organization structures;
- being innovative and initiating change – being 'animateurs';
- managing and utilizing increasingly sophisticated information systems;
- managing people with widely different and changing values and expectations.

Organizational and personal development in the organizations studied were in addition seen to depend on corporate cultures which encouraged openness, trust and involvement, and which encouraged initiative and continuous learning, even from failures. The personal qualities emphasized in this study include independence, openness to change, assertiveness, being a good motivator, having drive, and having tact.

From a study of changes affecting around 200 middle managers in eight organizations, Sue Dopson and Rosemary Stewart (1990) conclude that this group do indeed now face, 'a more turbulent environment which has frequently radically changed their role and function', in the following respects:

- More generalist with greater responsibilities and a wider range of tasks.
- Increasing span of control.
- Responsible for a wider mix of staff.

- More accountable.
- Performance is more visible, through computerization of management information.

Dopson and Stewart point out that their sample is limited, and that it may be unwise to generalize too widely from their data. Their overall conclusion, however, is that:

> The changes in middle management jobs had complex implications for middle managers themselves. They were required to change their managerial attitudes, and to acquire new skills. Greater flexibility and adaptability were stressed as were more generalist skills which included financial knowledge, a greater ability to manage staff and staff of different backgrounds, a wider understanding of what was happening around them both in other departments and outside, and a greater marketing and strategic orientation.
>
> In the organizations we studied middle managers were described as more important than in the past, both because in slimmer, flatter organizations, they have more responsibility, but mainly because they are seen by top management as occupying a pivotal role in implementing changes and thus able to influence the success or otherwise of the organization. (Dopson and Stewart, 1990, p. 13)

Summarizing evidence from survey work published by the British Institute of Management, Coulson-Thomas (1991, p. 3) argues: 'Organizations face an unprecedented range of challenges and opportunities in the social, economic, political and business environment. This external environment is characterized by uncertainty, surprise, turbulence and discontinuity.' Echoing the predictions of Burns and Stalker, Bennis, Toffler and Kanter, Coulson-Thomas points out that the survey data reveals the following trends:

- To survive in the face of multiple challenges, organizations have to become more flexible and responsive, incorporating systematic processes for continuous learning, adaptation and change.
- Work is increasingly delegated to multi-functional teams, with project management replacing traditional bureaucratic or hierarchical management.
- Organization structures are becoming flatter, and developing into networks, with computerized links to customers, suppliers and business partners.
- There is an increasing requirement for 'a new approach to management', with flexible access to expertise and a change-facilitating role for experts and specialists.

Coulson-Thomas (1991, p. 5) is thus able to argue further that 'Bureaucratic organizations are transitioning into more flexible forms, based upon teams', and variously describes these new organizational forms as 'the responsive organization', 'the network organization', and 'the flexible organization'. Project management is 'one of the key sets of facilitating skills which is emerging' in this analysis. Coulson-Thomas cites further data from a survey carried out for the Association of Project Managers claiming that the desired competences include understanding 'the anatomy of a project', communication, decision making, planning, scheduling and control, and contract management.

Michael McCaskey (1988) lists the management skills and attitudes that, he concludes from his research, are necessary for coping with change, ambiguity, flexible organization structures, and with poorly structured problems. This unusual list includes:

- *Problem finding* Ability to bring a combination of judgement, intuition and logic to the recognition of problems and opportunities.
- *Map-building* Ability to generate fresh ways of conceptualizing problem situations.
- *Janusian thinking* Ability constructively to join apparently contradictory views and beliefs (after the Roman god who faced in two directions simultaneously).
- *Controlling and not controlling* Adopting a 'posture of assertively going with the flow' – knowing when to exert influence, and when to let events take their course.
- *Humour that oils* Helping to regulate stress and encourage creativity – avoiding sarcasm and denigration – using the restorative power of laughter.
- *Charisma* Ability to stir enthusiasm, confidence and commitment in others.

McCaskey offers three other items of practical advice as follows for managing unstructured problems:

1. Establish a core team that is embedded in a network of contacts and information.
2. Adopt a flexible approach to planning, with the focus on 'domain and direction' rather than on specific measurable goals.
3. Establish *ad hoc* or temporary structures, such as task forces or project teams.

Networking, goal flexibility and temporary structures are issues to which we return at various points elsewhere in this text.

Obeng (1990) claims that companies are moving 'beyond matrix management' in using temporary project management teams to deal with complex tasks, and that project management skills are increasingly in demand as a result. Obeng also describes this as a shift to 'project-based management', and argues that 'the tools and principles of project management thus become an integral part of mainstream management'. These fluid structures in which projects, priorities and project team memberships are regularly overlapping and changing renders the project-based management role more demanding than a traditional line management job, in Obeng's view, particularly where the external environment is more unpredictable, time-scales are more open-ended, and progress monitoring is thus more complex.

He argues that 'not every project can be organized neatly and logically using various methods of planning and control'. Obeng thus concludes that project managers must think of themselves as change agents (see the discussion in Chapter 1 concerning our inability to distinguish between these two labels, for precisely this reason).

Obeng argues that four sets of skills are important. *Planning and controlling skills*, although long recognized, are still important. *Learning skills* are critical for working in unfamiliar settings, assimilating new information, and adjusting plans and priorities to meet changing conditions. *People skills* for negotiating, influencing, listening, and managing stakeholders are central, including what Obeng describes as managing 'the invisible team' of those involved in and affected – directly and indirectly – by change. Finally, the change agent requires *organizational skills* with respect to political sensitivity, awareness of wider organizational issues, and networking with other managers.

The available evidence and commentary thus suggest that there is at least some substance in the claim that increased environmental turbulence has led to the development of organic, fuzzy, fluid, adaptable and flexible organization structures, with consequent implications for management in general as well as for the effective management of change.

Organization type – crisp or fuzzy, mechanistic or organic – thus conditions the manner in which the change agent may have to proceed in order to introduce proposals effectively. The change agent is therefore advised to make this diagnosis before arriving at judgements concerning how to proceed. The structures and systems in a mechanistic and routinized organization will make demands on the competences of the change agent different from those likely to arise in an adaptable organic setting. This diagnosis will need to extend, in some settings, to a diagnosis of how the organization structures and systems themselves may be changing, or may have to change, say, from more rigid modes of operation to fuzzier systems; this can be seen as a continuum, and different sections of the same organization can be located at different points across that spectrum, depending on the environment they face and their preferred operational modes. The approach, techniques and style of the change agent thus have to vary from setting to setting; what is effective in one setting may not always be appropriate in another. This analysis reinforces the argument that the expertise of the change agent is dependent on context (a view expressed, for example, by the British Institute of Personnel Management on the Management Charter Initiative which seeks to identify a universal set of management competences).

Managing in quadrant four

At the end of the previous section, we offered an approach to classifying organizational type. How can we appropriately classify the nature of change itself?

For our purposes in exploring the necessary expertise of the change agent, we have not found the distinction between strategic and non-strategic change to be helpful. We have found it useful instead in management development settings to explore the nature of change on three other key dimensions, ignoring at this point the implications of environmental turbulence. These concern the perceived centrality of change to the primary task of the organization, the perceived scale of change, and the pace at which change is introduced. The primary task of the organization is the task it has to perform in order to survive. Leaving the pace of change aside temporarily, plotting organizational change on the first two of these dimensions creates the matrix in Figure 2.1.

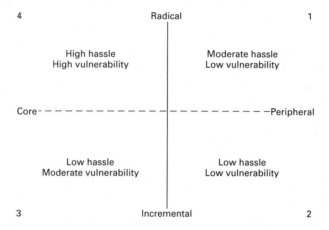

Figure 2.1   The four-quadrant model of organizational change

In quadrant one within Figure 2.1, change which is perceived as radical, but which is peripheral to the primary task of the organization, is likely to present the change agent with comparatively few implementation problems. The 'hassle factor' is likely to be moderate, in terms of the volume of frustrating, conflictual and time-consuming technical and organizational issues. Time-scales are likely to be relatively relaxed, and the penalities for error are likely to be similarly slight, consistent with the limited impact on the overall business of the organization. The changes are also likely to be reversible, or capable of deflection. This may be high budget change, but is likely to be under little pressure to rush things through, and the probability of error is reduced. The personal 'vulnerability' of the change agent is, therefore, likely to be low, in terms of the potential damage to the reputation and career prospects of the change agent, should things go wrong. The introduction of a new networked word processing and electronic mail system in a manufacturing organization could be an example of a quadrant one change; potentially a radical departure from existing systems and in its impact on those directly involved, but peripheral to the primary manufacturing task of the organization.

In quadrant two, change which is perceived as incremental and which is also peripheral to the primary task of the organization, is likely to present the change agent with even fewer implementation problems. In contrast with quadrant one, the hassle factor will probably be low. Time-scales are likely to be relatively unimportant and the penalties for error are likely to be minimal. The changes are again likely to be reversible, or at least capable of adaptation to meet specific complaints and interests. This may be low budget change, with little chance of error. The personal vulnerability of the change agent is, therefore, also very low. The change to a new generation of word processing software, or the introduction of a new job evaluation scheme and payment system for secretarial staff could be examples of quadrant two change; peripheral to the main business activity, and incremental in their departure from existing systems and procedures.

In quadrant three, change which is perceived as affecting the core of the organization's activity but which is an incremental departure from existing arrangements, is likely to present the change agent with significantly more implementation problems. To the extent that the content of the changes reflect incremental departures from current arrangements, the hassle factor may be low. However, time-scales and budgets are likely to come under more scrutiny, the changes are likely to be less easily reversed, and the penalities for error are likely to be higher than they are in the first two quadrants. The personal vulnerability of the change agent is, therefore, moderately high. The gradual introduction of cross-craft working in a multi-union manufacturing plant, or the upgrading of an existing management information system, could be examples of quadrant three change; affecting the conduct of the main business activity, but incremental in their departure from existing arrangements and systems.

In quadrant four, change which is perceived to affect the organization's core activity and which is seen as a radical departure from existing arrangements, is likely to present the change agent with multiple implementation problems – organizational and technical. The hassle factor is likely to be high. Time-scales and budgets are likely to be critical. The changes are likely to involve irreversible long-term commitments. The penalties for error will therefore be high. The personal vulnerability of the change agent is thus likely to be correspondingly high. The construction of a new, fully re-equipped machine shop, or the move to new and improved office accommodation, or merger with a complementary business 20 kilometers south, could all be examples of quadrant four changes; affecting the conduct of the primary task of the organization, and representing fundamental departures from existing conditions. This of course is the category of change which normally attracts the label 'strategic'.

This classification of organizational change into four types or quadrants requires at least four qualifications.

First, the pace or timing of change must also be considered. It is tempting to classify change on a continuum from rapid to slow. This, however, does not adequately express the reality of organizational change which typically proceeds through more or less rapid and more or less stagnant phases, depending on a number of factors, and in particular on the relative priority attached to a particular activity at any given time. Another appropriate dimension therefore concerns the relative stability or fluctuation of the pace of change. This dimension has particular significance in quadrant four, where pace and timing can critically influence perceptions of change and the support or resistance which it attracts.

Second, the categorization of change in this model is perceptual, and will differ from setting to setting. Change that is perceived as radical in one organization may be commonplace in another. Change peripheral to one organization will be core to another. It is the perceptions of those involved which are critical here. The attempt to define 'strategic change' from an outsider's perspective is, in this respect, awkward, if not irrelevant.

Third, change projects can 'migrate' from quadrant to quadrant. Perceptions and priorities shift, for a number of reasons, and change that was regarded as peripheral and incremental can develop and expand to have what are seen to be radical implications for the core activity of the organization. There appears to be anecdotal evidence to suggest that many information technology projects migrate in this way, as the 'strategic potential' of new systems is only slowly discovered in the implementation process. On the other hand, change that begins in quadrant four may not consistently be perceived to have the radical and core attributes with which the project began, and may migrate elsewhere.

Fourth, the vulnerability of the change agent across these four stereotyped settings has been set in negative terms, with respect to the price of error. The rewards which potentially attach to the change agent reflect the level of vulnerability. Few managers have built highly successful personal careers on a history of incremental and peripheral changes to their organizations. The successful change agent in a quadrant four setting is in contrast highly visible in the organization, with consequent implications for short-term reward and longer-term career prospects.

We are in this book concerned primarily with the management of change in quadrant four, recognizing that perceptions of change migrate over time for a number of reasons. Quadrant four, by definition, presents the change agent with the most problematic management context.

This is a subtly different approach to that adopted by commentators interested in the study of 'strategic change'. We earlier noted Pettigrew's (1987) attempt to define strategic change in terms of scale and scope. In the view advanced here, 'strategic' can be seen to equate with 'radical and core' and with quadrant four, but only with respect to the perceptions of organizational actors in a given context. Change thus may or may not become strategic in the perceptions of organizational actors irrespective of the categories of observers. This perspective is also consistent with the view that the evolution of organizational strategy tends to be incremental, rather than rapid and revolutionary (Quinn, 1980; Johnson, 1990).

We have up to this point indicated broadly the nature of the context facing the change agent – organic, turbulent, vulnerable. In the following sections, we will attempt to specify in more detail how this context presents itself to and is understood by the change agent. By exploring the 'phenomenological texture' of the change agent's context, we will seek to construct a more refined model of context, of the specific factors contributing to personal vulnerability, and thereby to establish the skills, abilities and competences required to function effectively.

We suggested at the end of the previous section that the change agent requires the diagnostic capability to determine organizational type, and how that type may be changing or need to be changed, in order to decide how effectively to proceed with change proposals. We can now add that the change agent also requires diagnostic capability to determine the nature of change in hand, in terms of the quadrant in our simple model to which it belongs, and also to determine how that categorization is or should be migrating through time.

The 'phenomenological texture' of context

How is the context of change experienced by the change agent? The focus of much research in this area has been with change, and not directly with the change agent. We will in this section report a study which sought to establish just this – to explore how the task of the project manager is influenced by aspects of context, using a two-stage approach to data collection (Buchanan, 1991). This first involved the production of 'audio diaries' by eight project managers, followed by a national survey which attracted 114 usable responses. The purpose of the diary approach was to generate 'fine grain' accounts of the personal experience of managing change. The purpose of the survey was to improve confidence in the generalizability of the diary findings.

The first stage of this research involved the recruitment of eight project managers who were asked to produce 'audio diaries' of their personal experiences of change management. These were tape-recorded narrative accounts of recent or current change programmes, generated according to a structured brief which respondents were asked to interpret according to their individual circumstances. Following an individual recruitment and briefing session, diarists were invited to a group briefing at which the aims of the project and the research procedure were explained. At these individual and group sessions, it was emphasized that the research was concerned with how change and context presented themselves to the change agent, and not with predefined concepts of change or any of its dimensions. Similarity of experience of organizational process and structures across these respondents and their employing organizations was not assumed. On the contrary, that experience was diverse. The research was instead concerned with commonalities in the phenomenological texture of change – or in straightforward language, with the nature of change as it is experienced by the change agent.

Diarists were asked to dictate on audio tape and in their own time during the two weeks following the initial briefing an account of their experience of managing change in accordance with the following instructions:

> We would like you to tell us the story of an organizational change programme, for which you have had a management responsibility, and which you feel has been a major learning experience for you. It is impossible to set a list of questions that would apply to every setting. So, we would like you to tell us the story of your change programme in a way that covers as many of these issues as you think appropriate:
>
> - What were the objectives of the change programme?
> - What was your role in the programme?
> - Was management responsibility shared?
> - What in your judgement were the 'critical incidents'?
> - What in your judgement were the main decision points?
> - What part have 'politics' played in this programme?
> - On what criteria can you assess the outcomes?
> - Are there any outstanding issues or problems?
> - What key aspects are not covered by these questions?
> - What for you are the main lessons?

The eight diarists were:

1. Chief Officer, probation service, concerned with the implementation of a new organization-wide management information system.
2. Engineering and Development Director, oil refining company, responsible for commissioning a new specialist oil refining plant from design and build to operation.
3. Business Manager, computer manufacturing, concerned with the development of a pan-European order fulfilment system affecting all company shipping locations in Europe.
4. Technical Director, engineering company, implementing computer-aided drafting covering three company operations.
5. Management Services Manager, local authority, concerned with a major policy change affecting workload and conditions in a key service area.
6. Systems Manager, public utility, implementing an enhanced computer system to maintain an asset register and a planned maintenance programme.
7. Logic Manager, electronics manufacturing, concerned with a major re-organization involving the integration of previously separate groups to exploit new market opportunities.
8. Director, land survey company, developing geographic information systems, and thereby diversifying into new markets.

This small sample includes a broad mix of traditional and 'high-tech' manufacturing, large and small companies, manufacturing and service organizations, and public and private sector concerns. These diarists were selected for their direct managerial involvement in radical changes affecting either their whole organization or a significant section of it. However, the small size and wide variation of this sample place clear limitations on the generalizability of the findings from the diary analysis.

The accounts were transcribed and returned to individual diarists for confirmation. This procedure generated approximately 50,000 words of transcribed accounts in total; only a proportion of the data set is reported and used here. The method of analysis of the diary transcripts was simple content analysis which involved identification of recurring main themes in response to specific questions addressed to the data set. Content analysis is a subjective classification procedure, the validity of which was monitored in this case through two mechanisms. First, the analysis was initially conducted independently by the two researchers, whose main points of disagreement concerned appropriate category labels. Second, the results were presented to respondents in a half-day debriefing session, during which they were invited to offer advice and criticism with respect to the findings and their implications. They confirmed the categories identified, but also indicated a 'missing category' which is elaborated below. Given the desire to highlight the practical management implications of this research, this check and elaboration on the 'validity in use' of the content analysis was significant.

The second stage of data collection concerned a short survey questionnaire published in a management services journal with national circulation and a wide readership, and which attracted 114 responses. The survey questions were in five sections, concerning the perceived importance of contextual issues, the relevance of management competences, reasons for not using competences in practice, blockages to effective project implementation, and background information. As with diary transcripts, only part of the data set is reported here.

Survey respondents came from the following range of management functions:

- Financial   6 per cent
- Personnel   15
- Engineering/computing   28
- Production   13
- Business planning   24
- Other   13

Six survey items were included to provide a broad overview of the kinds of changes experienced by respondents (See Table 2.2).

Of what management population is this sample representative? Those survey items in Table 2.2 indicate that the majority of respondents – at least two-thirds – were drawing on experience of radical and strategic change in answering this questionnaire, with less than 20 per cent disagreeing with the first three items. It appears that this sample shares some common experience with the eight audio diarists. However, radical change affecting the core of the business need not always be accompanied by the rapid commitment of resource to 'state of the art' ideas and techniques. Change in quadrant four, therefore, is not necessarily fast-

Table 2.2 An overview of the kinds of changes experienced by respondents to the journal questionnaire.

	Agree %	*Neutral* %	*Disagree* %
The project is closely aligned to the strategic direction of the organization.	70	22	8
It involves radical technical and/or organizational change.	69	17	12
The change is intended to have a radical effect on the core activities of the organization.	64	17	18
We intend to introduce the changes rapidly.	49	25	25
The project is based on 'state of the art' thinking.	42	35	23
A significant amount of additional financial and staffing resources will be needed.	32	28	40

paced. Less than half the sample expressed agreement with the second three items, with which 23 to 40 per cent of respondents disagreed. This raises again the problem introduced in Chapter 1 concerning how distinctions can be made between 'strategic' and other types of change.

The context of change

The eight diary transcripts were first analysed, using the validity monitoring procedure outlined above, by separating and content analysing entries relating to the context of the changes described by the diarists. Pettigrew's (1987) distinction between the inner and outer context of change offers an intuitively appealing categorization. However, this proved inadequate to capture the dimensions on which the context of change was experienced by the audio diarists. The following three context issues initially emerged from the transcript analysis:

1. Interlocking.
2. Shifting sands.
3. Ownership.

Interlocking

The diary entries made frequent reference to how implementation can be assisted or impeded by a range of interdependencies. This typically concerns managers and staff in other sections and divisions of the organization, other organizations, and suppliers of technology. Typical examples of the problems of interlocking are as follows:

- Waiting for decisions and actions to be taken in other divisions of the organization.
- Attempting to combine company with vendor expertise to satisfy the needs of a major customer.
- Adopting a new system that will be used by three major but separate departments in the organization.

One illustration of interlocking decisions comes from this entry in the diary of the Logic Manager, electronics manufacturing company:

> With marketing now no longer actively seeking cell-based or full custom work for the plant, and refusing to process customer enquiries, the situation was essentially a stalemate. The US management were not prepared to get involved, viewing the position as a European one. This could partly be explained by the fact that there was no direct reporting link to the US vice president, rather marketing reported to the European general manager based in Munich. Also, the Business Centre manager was in a much stronger position relative to our Design Manager.

This diary entry from a Systems Manager illustrates the problems generated by a multi-purpose system straddling various organizational functions and divisions in a public utility:

> This project is concerned with developing an enhanced computer system which is intended to maintain an asset register of equipment requiring maintenance by a distribution engineering department and involves taking information from a computer system developed some years ago, improving the quality of data on that system, and transferring it over to the new system. At the same time, the new system is intended to carry out our maintenance scheduling of periodic routine maintenance together with recording instances of non-routine breakdown or emergency type maintenance required in addition to retaining maintenance history job records.
>
> A major feature of this system is to be the automatic generation of job instructions from a database reading the maintenance over a five-year period. In other words, the computer is intended to read all the maintenance schedules that have been input and give advanced generation of the job documents so that they are issued to the correct workplace in something like two weeks in advance of when the actual plan date for the maintenance occurs.

The change agent thus has to identify and coordinate these varying linkages, to establish and sustain coherence across changing networks of people and attitudes, to anticipate how action in one domain will impact others. Some of these potential linkages are clear and obvious, while others are uncertain and difficult to predict.

Shifting sands

The diary accounts made frequent reference to changes in the inner and outer contexts of the organization affecting the project implementation. These changes were typically interrelated, unpredictable, and outwith the control of the change agent, but impacted on change processes in obvious and subtle ways. Typical examples of 'shifting sands' included changes in:

- market conditions, suppliers and customers;
- management perceptions of market and organizational needs;
- technological developments;
- organization structure;
- key managers and management positions.

Change in these circumstances can be less project driven and may be more appropriately conceived as 'programmatic', as indicated earlier in this chapter, and as the Logic Manager from the electronics manufacturing company observed:

In 1983, semiconductor analysts, enthused by the prospect of an applications specific integrated circuit revolution, projected a billion dollar market by 1988, growing to a $20 billion business by 1990. In response, we decided to reorganize and form a specific division to tackle this market. This reorganization demanded the integration of various groups whose culture, values and skills varied extensively. The change is not a project as such, with a predefined start and end, but rather is a programme of continuous change.

Another example of the way in which changing priorities and goals affect the change agent comes from this diary entry from the Chief Officer, probation service:

Just coming back from 'Managing the '90s Action Group' meeting where we have been discussing our action plans. A useful meeting. Mostly the people there particularly concerned about the County Council Senior Management Review which will have a significant effect on them as individuals as well as their organizations. The uncertainty that it is generating means that they really don't know what their job will be in six months time or indeed in some cases whether they will actually have one. That tended to mean that their action plans have gone out the window as they consider survival. That may be short-sighted in some ways, but perhaps inevitable.

The change agent thus has to be able to 'shift with the sands' as conditions, objectives and priorities change with changing technologies, markets, and organization structures.

Ownership

Responsibility for project management is sometimes unclear, may involve several individuals, and can change during the life of a project. There can be confusion and uncertainty about specific responsibilities for actions during implementation, and there can be further ambiguity about ultimate management responsibility for new systems and divisions.

Aspects of this problem are illustrated by the diary entry from the Engineering and Development Director in the oil refining company, which was a medium-size family business at the time of this research:

> During the very difficult commissioning period, it was apparent that the Managing Director of the company, himself having some technical bias, had formed a view that most of the problems were technical and that it was necessary to bring in certain consultants to help us overcome the difficulties. None of these consultants were especially helpful, with the exception of one retired American gentleman, who offered fairly sound advice, although by the time he appeared we had already established good working practices for the plant.
>
> Nonetheless, this idea of technical restrictions on the project did appear to me at least to be uppermost in the mind of the Managing Director and he allowed his son [also a Director] to recruit a senior manager from a major oil company. The new man was brought in to become Operations and Technical Director. The Managing Director's son had by that time become Managing Director, and his father became Chairman of the company.

This kind of confusion of responsibilities is not confined to medium-size family companies. The Technical Director of the engineering company in one diary entry describes how:

> The management responsibility was primarily placed on the Electric Controls Manager, although there was also some responsibility placed on the individual Department Managers who use the system within their own departments once they had been introduced to the system's capabilities. The

range of these responsibilities was vague and there was no division of responsibility until the equipment had been introduced and initial training had taken place.

These three key dimensions – interlocking, shifting sands and ownership – appear to characterize the organizational context in which the change agent functions, as viewed from the individual manager's perspective. This account emphasizes context factors and potentially portrays the change agent in a wholly reactive mode, responding to and constrained by these issues. This is a partial picture and the scope for proaction is varied, anticipating the implications of particular dimensions of and events in the context and acting to alter or deflect those when possible and as appropriate.

Confirmation of the influence of these three context factors on the role of the change agent was sought in the survey data which presents a different set of findings, and which describes a fourth factor indicated, as explained above, by the audio diarists during debriefing. Respondents were asked to rate their agreement with a series of statements describing various ways in which, in their view, the context of change affected the management process.

Table 2.3 Respondents' assessment of the effect on the management process of 'interlocking' context issues

	Agree %	Neutral %	Disagree %
The project is likely to have a lot of repercussions around the organization.	78	17	5
Success will depend heavily on consequential changes elsewhere in the organization.	55	24	21
Success will depend on supporting changes being made by third parties such as suppliers.	43	20	37

Statements related to *interlocking* issues received the replies listed in Table 2.3. These replies support the view that the change agent has to be alert to the 'ripple effects' of change elsewhere in the organization. However, the degree of project dependency on related changes and third parties appears to vary considerably. This feature of the context is thus likely to be experienced in different ways by different change agents, and the appropriate responses when faced with such differing pressures and contexts will vary.

Statements related to *shifting sands* issues received the replies listed in Table 2.4. Only three of the seven items in this category attracted agreement from more than half the sample. These relate to new opportunities, the fickleness of support, and uncertainty over the best means to achieve the project ends. Problems created by changing project objectives seem to have been experienced by less than half this sample, with a quarter to a third of respondents indicating that they did not

Table 2.4   Respondents' assessment of the effect on the management process of 'shifting sands' context issues

	Agree %	Neutral %	Disagree %
People tend to back away when the change runs into difficulties.	68	21	11
The changes are expected to open up new strategic opportunities for the organization.	60	25	15
There is some uncertainty about the best way of achieving objectives of the change.	53	28	19
People are tempted to take short cuts to get changes introduced.	48	23	19
Different factions in the organization regularly propose different goals for the change.	47	28	25
The volatile environment has led to alterations in the original objectives.	44	26	30
Changes elsewhere lead people to suggest different objectives for the project.	42	35	23

face such alterations to their objectives. These findings again highlight the partiality of the picture generated from simple content analysis of the unrepresentative small-sample diary data.

Table 2.5   Respondents' assessment of the effect on the management process of 'ownership' context issues.

	Agree %	Neutral %	Disagree %
It is not always clear who 'owns' the change.	58	24	18
Since the change involves different groups, it is sometimes difficult to know who is really taking responsibility for it.	48	15	37

Statements related to *ownership* issues received the replies listed in Table 2.5. As with the previous two context issues, experience here is varied. It appears from the replies on the second of these items, where 85 per cent have either agreed or disagreed with 15 per cent 'neutral', that experience here may depend on organizational practice, perhaps with respect to job definition and the clarity with which role boundaries are drawn. (Andersen *et al.*, 1988, emphasise clarity, precision, planning, targets and the use of a 'responsibility chart' to avoid role ambiguity – following conventional project management advice.)

In the debriefing meeting with audio diarists, a fourth set of context issues of 'managing up' were expressed, concerning the perceptions of and relationships with senior managers in the organization and the way in which these factors affected the role of the change agent. These issues did arise in the diary accounts, but had not initially emerged as a separate theme in the search for context issues. The diarists subsequently argued that this lack of emphasis was not representative of their wider experience, and items were added to the survey questionnaire to explore this further. The results indicate the importance of 'senior management stance' as a fourth major context issue.

Table 2.6 Respondents' assessment of the effect on the management process of 'senior stance' context issues

	Agree %	Neutral %	Disagree %
Senior management is expecting quick results.	66	20	14
Some senior managers have unrealistic expectations about the project and what it is likely to achieve.	50	31	19
Senior management does not appreciate the challenge which the project involves.	46	21	33

Statements related to *senior stance* received the replies listed in Table 2.6. In a subsequent section of the questionnaire, 79 per cent of respondents rated 'top managers not providing enough commitment and support' as one of the key reasons why projects often run into difficulties.

The vulnerable change agent

In order to establish the priorities of the change agent in terms of areas of attention and action, it is clearly important to consider the wider context in which this activity takes place, and to take into account the variation in that context, across projects and through time. From the diary and survey findings it is possible to identify for analytical purposes two extreme contexts, in which the change agent is exposed to high and low levels of 'vulnerability' respectively. Here vulnerability refers to the scale and complexity of the problems facing the change agent, the degree of uncertainty and risk involved, and to the anticipated degree of contention and resistance which the change is likely to generate. Given that the context experienced by the change agent can vary between these extreme positions, and that the context can alter through time, the two extremes are summarized in Table 2.7.

Table 2.7   High and low vulnerability context features

High vulnerability context	*Low vulnerability context*
Strategic changes	Operational changes
Rapid change, quick results	Slow change, slow results
Significant resource commitment	Few extra resources needed
Disinterested top management	Supportive top managers
Unrealistic top management expectations	Realistic top management expectations
Fickle support	Solid support
Uncertain means	Certainty of means
Complex interdependencies	Few interdependencies
Dependent on third parties	Independent
Multiple 'ripples'	Self-contained
Conflicting perceptions	Shared views
Multi-purpose changes	Single-function systems
Unstable goals	Stable goals
Confused responsibilities for process and outcomes	Clear 'ownership' of process and outcomes

In the light of our earlier discussion of how change may be categorized, the low vulnerability context specified in Table 2.7 equates with the situation facing the change agent in quadrants one and two, where change is peripheral to the core activity of the business and is thus less contentious. Quadrant one, involving radical departures from established arrangements, may tend towards some attributes of a higher vulnerability context. In contrast, the high vulnerability context equates more closely with the situation facing the change agent in quadrants three and four. This mapping, however, is not so straightforward. The factors which influence the vulnerability of the change agent go beyond the scale of change and its relationship with the core business. Vulnerability is also affected, in this perspective, by the views and expectations of top management, by the nature of the problem, and by the nature of the resources available to the change agent – including commitment and support.

Many, if not all, of the characteristics of the high vulnerability context as identified here are also likely to be found in organizations which have developed organic or fuzzy structures, as discussed earlier in this chapter. Project-based management, and the expertise related to such roles, can thus be expected to become critical to the performance of the middle management function and the work of change agents in such organizational settings. Once again, however, there is not a perfect overlap between high vulnerability contexts and organic management systems.

Vulnerability and agenda

The 'high vulnerability' context is described here in what could be seen as derogatory terms. However, the pressures on the change in both contexts can be extreme, albeit for different reasons, and the satisfactions and rewards in both contexts can also be substantial.

As noted in Chapter 1, conventional project management texts have concentrated on the 'content' and 'control' agendas of the change agent, offering process advice based on a rational-linear view of organizational change. This view emphasizes 'technical' expertise in the substance of the change, and the need for project planning capabilities (mainly concerned with critical path analysis, timing, budgeting and progress monitoring). Sociological analyses have in contrast tended to marginalize these content and control issues, seeing them as insignificant in relation to the political, symbolic and ritualistic aspects of the role of the change agent. Here the emphasis is on the process agenda and on the ability of the change agent to influence the political and cultural systems of the organization.

The findings presented here offer a different view of the role of the change agent and of the diagnostic skills required in this position. In terms of priorities, it would appear that in a 'low vulnerability context' the allocation of priorities across the three agendas to which the change agent must pay attention will typically be:

1. Content.
2. Control.
3. Process.

Managing the process of change in this context appears unproblematic, or less problematic. Change is more likely to proceed in a logically sequenced manner without significant deflection, and in the comparative absence of political issues. Issues of project control are likely to be comparatively relaxed, the change agent can concentrate on content or 'technical' issues (whether this is advanced manufacturing technology or a new approach to work organization and rewards systems), and is likely to have been chosen for the task on the basis of prior qualifications and expertise in the substance of the changes. Rewards are likely to be assessed on the basis of technical competence and achievements and not on managerial successes. A rational-linear view of the change process is more likely to reflect the reality as experienced by the change agent and as perceived by other organizational actors, and advice set in that frame is more likely to be appropriate. The process agenda cannot be ignored, but is likely to make fewer demands on the resources and competences of the change agent.

However, in a 'high vulnerability context', the allocation of priorities across the three project agendas may be reversed:

1. Process.
2. Control.
3. Content.

Managing the process of change in this context is highly problematic, for the individual change agent and for the organization. Here the control agenda remains important, given the likely levels of senior management scrutiny and the high visibility of the project activity. In this context, however, rewards are likely to be assessed on the basis of managerial achievements, not on technical competence and successes, and competence in managing the process agenda becomes more significant. A rational-linear view of the change process and advice set in that frame are less likely to be perceived relevant. The change agent may be under pressure to ensure that the process is seen in the organization to proceed in a logically sequenced manner, but this is likely to be supported and sustained by much 'back stage decision-making' (Pettigrew, 1985, p. 438). The content agenda cannot be ignored, but the change agent may be better advised to direct resources and attention to the other two agendas and to rely on the technical expertise available in the project support group.

Two other survey items support this argument. First, 86 per cent of respondents rate the need for project leaders to have the right skills mix (technical, business, interpersonal) as very important or important, with only 14 per cent expressing disagreement. Second, the question which asks respondents for their view of the statement, 'It is sometimes said that major change projects need now to be managed by people who can combine technical expertise, business awareness and interpersonal skill, rather than by those whose abilities are primarily technical', attracts 100 per cent agreement.

Hamilton (1988) also argues the importance of management skills over technical competence, concluding that 'computer illiterate change agents' may be appropriate and effective in some contexts. The British Computer Society has recently launched an initiative designed to improve education and training for computing professionals, to increase the number of 'hybrid' managers who are able to combine information technology expertise with business awareness and management skills (Palmer and Ottley, 1990; Earl and Skyrme, 1990).

The context in which the change agent functions thus varies from setting to setting, from project to project, and across time, generating differential demands on management skills and action. The available literature does not always recognize this variation, or is not helpful in relating project management practice to different context patterns. The characterization of context patterns here is not meant to deny variation in the area between the two extremes. The aim in this approach has been to highlight the contrasting pressures and demands facing the change agent in different settings, and to offer guidance to those seeking practical management advice from the apparently inconsistent literatures on the subject.

Contextual variation implies differential selection and appraisal criteria for change agents. It would appear prudent to select managers with content and control expertise for low vulnerability contexts where the skills required to manage the process agenda are less significant. Change agents in this context may realistically expect to be appraised on their technical competence, and on their ability to manage the implementation in accordance with time and resource budgets.

In high vulnerability contexts, technical expertise is comparatively less important, and it would appear prudent to select managers who can combine knowledge of project planning and control techniques with 'power skills' in mobilising support, negotiating resources, communications, stimulating enthusiasm, and overcoming and blocking resistance. Change agents in this context may realistically expect to be appraised on their ability to implement and stabilize a programme of change with widespread organizational support, rather than on their technical competence.

From the individual's perspective, the change agent with technical expertise and competence in control techniques but lacking process skills would be better advised to avoid high vulnerability contexts or seek appropriate training. The change agent weak in technical expertise, however competent in the control agenda, but adept in process skills should avoid low vulnerability contexts where content deficiencies are likely to be exposed, and seek career advancement in high vulnerability roles.

Management development programmes for change agents should also take into account context expectations, with managerial 'power skills' given more prominence for those expected to encounter high vulnerability contexts. Many project management development courses concentrate on control agenda techniques which, while useful, will not adequately equip all change agents with the broader-based competences they require. We will return to these issues in Chapter 5.

Events may lead to the migration of context along the multiple continua between the extremes of high and low vulnerability for the change agent. Regardless of the prevailing context, it may be useful to train change agents in diagnostic skills to assist in evaluating these shifts, to change agenda priorities, to widen their behaviour repertoire, and to adopt context-relevant strategies where possible.

As indicated in the opening section of this chapter, it is not always possible, or indeed helpful, to attempt to identify change as strategic, or non-strategic, for at least two reasons. First, such a classification is dependent on the perceptions of senior management; what is seen as strategic in one organization may be viewed differently elsewhere, with different implications for the change agent promoting or championing a particular line of action. Second, those perceptions themselves change; what was seen as a series of operational improvements last month can be recognized as having strategic import tomorrow, again with changing implications for the position and role of the change agent.

What is of more direct interest to the change agent, in terms of pressures and demands and appropriate strategies, is:

- the quadrant in which the change is perceived to lie; and
- the impact of interlocking, shifting sands, ownership and senior management view issues on vulnerability.

We have conducted this discussion in the absence of any clear statement of the precise skills implications for the change agent, particularly in a high vulnerability context, beyond identifying the importance of the process agenda. In Chapter 3, we will explore in more detail the nature of the change process which emerges from the perspective developed here, and we will return in Chapter 4 to an examination of the competence implications, with particular emphasis on process competences.

We have in this chapter emphasized the diagnostic requirements of the change agent. In summary, we have identified three, concerning respectively the need to diagnose the following aspects:

1. The type of organizational setting – mechanistic or organic – and how that is changing or may need to change.
2. The nature of the change proposals in hand – in terms of location on the quadrants model – and how that location could or should migrate to other quadrants.
3. The nature of the personal vulnerability of the change agent, and the implications for agenda priorities.

Our understanding of the expertise of the change agent thus has to be set in the framework of these diagnostic capabilities, which lead in turn to judgements about how most effectively and appropriately to proceed in the context, and to the deployment of specific competences in the pursuit of the change agent's goals.

3

Models of process

The private and public languages of change

Before beginning to engage in the political process, it is especially important to honestly consider the *private language* version of your values in relation to the changes you desire to implement. Other actors around you will see through your *public language*. If they do not find the outcome you desire to be congruent with their personal values, your public language will not ring true to them. They will look very carefully for private language interpretations of what you want. 'The best strategy for the company' will quickly be seen by others as simply best to advance your career or nothing more than your personal preference. Even when others may agree with the outcome you prefer, they will still be aware of the private language interpretation as well as the public language interpretation. They will know what is in it for you. Thus it is important to be able to view your preferred outcomes from the point of view of others to see how they will react. In fully considering the private language, you will also better understand the full range of your own motivations. [Italics added] (Graham, 1985, p. 214)

Logical sequence versus messy cocktail

The David Gleicher change formula is as follows:

Change will occur when K $\times$ D $\times$ V > C, where:

  K represents Knowledge of first practical steps
  D represents Dissatisfaction with the status quo
  V represents the desirable Vision of the future
  C represents the Cost (material and psychological) of movement.

(Source: David Gleicher of Arthur D. Little)

In this chapter, we will explore models of the process of change, concentrating in particular on models that depart from the conventional project management perspective and which focus on the social and political dynamics of organizational change. We will also consider the practical implications for the change agent in these perspectives. Clearly the nature of the change process is fundamental to understanding the demands made on the change agent and the consequences for skills development. One of the main issues that we wish to establish in this chapter is that the competences required of the change agent cannot be understood or expressed independently of the process of change which, following our analysis in Chapter 2, can be seen in turn to depend on characteristics of the context into which change is introduced. One of the main recurring themes in the models of the process of change examined here concerns the extent to which the change agent is required to resort to manipulative and devious behaviour. This is not the image of the open, communicative, caring, involving and understanding change agent portrayed in the participative management literature.

We discussed in Chapter 1 sociological accounts of organizational change where the implied rationality and linearity of the process were challenged. Rational-linear models of change have long since been discredited as descriptions or as explanations of organizational change, and thus also as guides to practical management action. We will, however, seek to demonstrate that this rejection is premature and that such models serve a symbolic, ritualistic, legitimating role for the change agent in certain contexts. The expertise of the change agent, particularly in organic, high-vulnerability contexts, is reflected in the parallel and complementary management of the unfolding logics of problem solving, ownership and legitimation. A number of commentators, such as Quinn (1980; 1982), have argued that organizational change is a blend of the analytic and political, and that strategic or radical change in particular is an incremental process of building support and commitment and of establishing legitimacy for new ideas. Quinn (1980) seeks to show how this involves setting broad goals and directions and letting the details emerge, probing, experimenting and learning in a conscious, purposeful and proactive way – incremental and logical at the same time. From this stance, the project management concerns with the content and control of change, the participative management concerns with ownership, and the sociological concern with legitimacy, can all be seen as partial, either as explanations of change or as guides to action.

James Brian Quinn (1980) argues that the 'formal planning' and 'power-behavioural' approaches to the analysis of change in organizations each offer critical insights, but are each limited, and that a synthesis of these approaches is required to approximate more closely to what in reality takes place. Logical decision making is constrained by cognitive limits, while 'power-political interplays' are contingent on what Quinn calls 'process limits' – that is, the timing and sequencing imperatives necessary to create awareness, build comfort levels, develop consensus, and select and train people' (Quinn, 1980, p. 51). The second half of the book is mainly a practical guide to 'managing logical incrementalism', in which the most important management processes are identified (p. 146) as:

- sensing needs
- amplifying understanding
- building awareness
- creating credibility
- legitimizing viewpoints
- generating partial solutions
- broadening support
- identifying zones of indifference and opposition
- changing perceived risks
- structuring needed flexibilities
- putting forward trial concepts
- creating pockets of commitment
- eliminating undesired options
- crystallizing focus and consensus
- managing coalitions
- formalizing agreed commitments

Quinn points out that the management techniques he identifies are 'not quite the textbook variety' (1980, p. 91). For example, broadening support for change proposals can be achieved through consultation, or selling, and by 'redundancy' of argument – that is through the persistent repetition of the case to reinforce the position. The creation of flexibility may involve encouraging 'activists' in the organization to move opportunistically, and may also involve 'systematic waiting', to see what happens, until someone retires or leaves or is promoted, or perhaps until a related project fails or succeeds. The elimination of undesired options, Quinn suggests, can be achieved effectively through the covert and selective encouragement or discouragement of the options and proposals raised by subordinates. In this way, the visible intervention of more senior management can be avoided.

Andrew Pettigrew (1985; 1987; 1988) has been a major British contributor to thinking in this area. Pettigrew, with Quinn, sees the process of change in organizations not as a logical, linear process but as an untidy cocktail of quests for power, competing views, rational assessment and manipulation, combined with the 'subtle processes of additively building up a momentum of support for change and then vigorously implementing change' (Pettigrew, 1985, p. xviii). He notes the growing distrust of 'formalized strategic planning procedures' and 'an increased sensitivity to more informal processes of leadership, vision building, and to team and commitment building as sufficient conditions to manage processes of creating strategic change' (Pettigrew, 1988, p. 2). He depicts strategic change as:

in essence a long-term conditioning, educating, and influence process designed to establish the dominating legitimacy of a different pattern of relations between strategic context and content . . . . (Pettigrew, 1985, p. 455)

Pettigrew, with numerous other contemporary management commentators, points out that the organization's capacity to adjust and adapt to change is a key factor in determining competitiveness. He claims that 'The management of strategic change is one of the central practical and theoretical issues of the 1980s' (Pettigrew, 1988, p. 1) and cites survey evidence which concluded that, in the mid-1980s, strategic planning and implementation was the most time-consuming activity demanding the personal attention of American chief executive officers.

Pettigrew offers a 'processual' and 'contextual' view of change. The context influences or shapes the how and why of change, and the tradition, culture, structure, business sector and socio-economic environment of the organization also constrain and facilitate change processes. Pettigrew's concern is thus with the process of change in context. Business and economic crises can be seen to precipitate change, with radical crises triggering radical change. Pettigrew is at pains to add, however, that internal organizational change cannot be explained simply by reference to such external events, and draws attention to the significance of 'processes of managerial perception, choice and action' (Pettigrew, 1985, p. xix). The ways in which managers and change agents perceive events and people are more significant than how these people and events are seen by other spectators.

Pettigrew is concerned with 'strategic change' in organizations, where the label 'strategic' is, in his terms 'just a description of magnitude'. Critical of the superficiality in rational-linear models, Pettigrew argues that:

> the real problem of strategic change is anchoring new concepts of reality, new issues for attention, new ideas for debate and resolution, and mobilising concern, energy and enthusiasm often in an additive and evolutionary fashion to ensure these early illegitimate thoughts gain powerful support and eventually result in contextually appropriate action. (Pettigrew, 1985, p. 438)

By defining 'the real problem of change' in these terms, Pettigrew clearly places quite a different set of items on the agenda of the change agent from those typically found in project management texts. The concerns with involvement and ownership expressed in the participative management literature acquire different connotations in the attempt to stimulate debate, and to mobilize concern. The emphases on goals, responsibilities, deadlines, controls and sympathetic involvement are here displaced by the concern with legitimacy:

> A central concept linking political and cultural analyses particularly germane to the understanding of continuity and change is legitimacy. The management of meaning refers to a process of symbol construction and value use designed to create legitimacy for one's ideas, actions, and demands, and to delegitimize the demands of one's opponents. Key concepts for analysing these processes of legitimization and delegitimization are symbolism, language, ideology and myth. (Pettigrew, 1985, p. 442)

The context and process of change are closely interrelated. Contextual events and characteristics trigger and legitimate change, and also facilitate and constrain certain aspects of the change implementation process. Compare the upgrading of the computerized personnel records and payroll system in a university with the development of a new computerized management information system for a retail chain store. The latter is likely to be in quadrant four – radical change central to business strategy and triggered by competitors' behaviour – while the personnel application represents an incremental improvement to an existing system peripheral to the core business of the institution based on internal considerations independent of what 'the competition' may or may not be doing in this respect. The process of change and the role of the change agent in these two contrasting settings are likely to be quite different. The process through which the change agent in the university context has to work with respect to establishing the legitimacy of the change proposals and justifying the investment is quite different from that facing the change agent in the retail store (although both will complain, if asked, about much the same general issues – scepticism from colleagues, lack of real interest from top management, no immediate or clear rewards for the effort involved, and so on).

The role of the change agent in Pettigrew's perspective is partly reactive – responding to environmental or contextual threats and opportunities – and partly proactive in exploiting contextual issues to promote change. Pettigrew seeks to illustrate how 'executive leadership' adjusts and interferes with strategy, structures, culture and political processes in the organization in order to focus attention on the need for change, and 'to create a different pattern of alignment between its internal character, strategy, and structure and the emerging views of its operating environment' (Pettigrew, 1985, p. xix).

However, Pettigrew's perspective also seeks to demonstrate how rational-analytical and political-cultural processes in the organization are interrelated. It is not appropriate to consider change as either rational or political; the processes of change in organizations incorporate both of these components. Echoing the distinction made by Graham (1985) between the private and the public languages in which change proposals are expressed, Pettigrew suggests that formal organizational procedures for proposing and justifying change are important, but that:

> Although on the surface the custom and practice of persuasion may dictate that initiatives for change are publicly justified on the weight of technical evidence and analysis, or more narrowly in terms of managerial drives for efficiency and effectiveness, it is too narrow to see change just as a rational and linear problem-solving process. (Pettigrew, 1987, p. 658)

Pettigrew had earlier expressed the same argument, about the distinction between public moves to support change and the 'behind the scenes' moves, in slightly different terms:

on the surface the custom and practice of persuasion may dictate that
initiatives for change are publicly justified ... Rather changes are also a
product of processes which recognize historical and continuing struggles for
power and status as motive forces, and consider which interest groups and
individuals may gain and lose as proposed changes surface, receive attention,
are consolidated and implemented, or fall from grace before they ever get off
the ground. (Pettigrew, 1985, p. 27)

The content of strategic change is thus ultimately a product of a legitimization
process shaped by political/cultural considerations, though often expressed in
rational/analytical terms. This recognition that intervening in an organization
to create strategic change is likely to be a challenge to the dominant ideology,
culture, and systems of meaning and interpretation, as well as the structures,
priorities, and power relationships of the organization, makes it clearer why
and how the processes of sensing, justifying, creating, and stabilizing
strategic change can be so tortuous and long. (Pettigrew, 1985, p. 443)

This clearly suggests both a tension and a separation between the *public*
performance of the change agent in justifying action in a manner acceptable to and
credible in the organization, and the private or *backstage* activity in drawing
attention to, establishing discussion around, and marshalling support for change.
Reinforcing this view, Pettigrew also states that:

Understanding strategic changes as continuous processes, with no clear
beginning or end, allows for the analysis of both discrete and identifiable
decision events, the pathways to and outcomes of those events – what may be
called the front stage of decision making; and indeed the back stage of
decision making, the processes by which novel ideas for change gain
currency and legitimacy in the organization, or are otherwise suppressed and
immobilized and never reach a form where they can be openly debated,
decided, and acted upon. (Pettigrew, 1985, p. 438)

The research agenda derived from this perspective involves longitudinal study of
organizational transformations, involving relationships between the three classes of
variables concerning content (what), context (why) and process (how). Longitudinal processual, contextual, and historical research in this area is rare, and
Pettigrew draws attention to this gap. It should be noted that such research is
difficult to mount and sustain, is resource intensive, and demands high levels of
commitment from researchers and host organizations. The payoff from such
research, however, is likely to be correspondingly fascinating and significant.

At some points in his analysis, Pettigrew appears to marginalize the role of the
change agent, subordinating the significance of the position to wider organizational
and environmental forces. He argues that it is necessary:

to conceptualize major transformations of the firm in terms of linkages between the content of change and its context and process and to regard leadership behaviour as a central ingredient but only one of the ingredients in a complex analytical, political, and cultural process of challenging and changing the core beliefs, structure, and strategy of the firm. (Pettigrew, 1987, p. 650)

However, he also emphasizes that, from his study of change in the British chemicals company ICI, 'All these cases indicate the importance in managerial terms of strong, persistent, and continuing leadership to create strategic change' (Pettigrew, 1985, p. 454). The leadership role here is concerned with articulating the issues that need to be tackled, with defining the problems to be considered important, with 'problem finding' in the first place, and with 'visionary presentation' of plans and ideas, often in imprecise ways.

Pettigrew does not, therefore, deny the importance of the role of the change agent, of visionary leadership, or of political and symbolic action in promoting and driving change. He is, however, concerned to locate that action firmly in the wider organizational and environmental context which both constrain and facilitate the actions of the change agent. The key role of 'exceptional people' has to be balanced with an understanding of the 'extraordinary circumstances' in which they find themselves acting.

Pettigrew is nevertheless critical of the way in which research in this field typically overlooks the significance of historical, contextual and processual issues in change management, abstracting change from the contextual factors which give it purpose, form and dynamic. It is the combination of contextual issues and crises with personal enthusiasm and drive that determine the nature and pace of change. The absence of change, Pettigrew argues, is typically due to a combination of absence of business pressure and lack of the 'energy and tension for change', which are derived from 'the vitality, imagination, visionary ideas and persistence of a leader championing a particular strategic change' (Pettigrew, 1985, p. 455). He thus advises against seeking 'the singular theory' of change, either with respect to the individual manager or to the context, and points instead to the 'political and cultural mosaic' which contribute to the multiplicity of factors and causes contributing to patterns of organizational change.

The skills of the change agent in Pettigrew's analysis thus concern the ability to intervene in the political and cultural systems of the organization, and the ability simultaneously to manage the content, context and process of change.

What are the implications of the view that the 'management of meaning' is central to the change process? From a practical point of view, what precisely does it mean to 'intervene in the organization's political and cultural systems'? What is involved in the 'simultaneous management of the content, context and process of change' – not to mention regulating the relationships between these three sets of factors? What is the value to the practising change agent of this 'processual and contextualist' perspective on organizational change? The richness of Pettigrew's formulation is in turn a potential weakness. Argyris (1988) is critical of this work precisely because, while it offers attractive tools for analysis and understanding, it offers little in the way of practical tools for action. He argues that 'although it is possible to use these comprehensive studies to alert practitioners to important factors to which they must attend, more work is required by scholars to show us how their propositions about understanding can be translated into propositions about taking action' (Argyris, 1988, p. 350).

Jane Dutton (1988), in exploring how attention becomes allocated to strategic issues, identifies specific tactics for manipulating the meaning – or 'orchestrating the impressions' – attached to management proposals. These concern *issue salience*, *issue sponsorship*, and *agenda structure*. Dutton's analysis can thus be used to add practical contours to Pettigrew's theoretical frame.

There are, for example, four sets of tactics that can be used to alter *issue salience*. The *magnitude* of an issue can be manipulated, perhaps by describing it as critical to survival, competitiveness, profitability or to other key organizational goals. The *abstractness* of the issue can be changed by grounding or by clouding it, by generalizing the issue to broaden support in some cases, or by making the issues more specific and focused in others. The *simplicity* of the issue can be manipulated, either by 'going to the heart of the matter', or by relating it in more complex ways to other concerns. The *immediacy* of the issue can be manipulated, making it a pressing concern to stimulate action, or by playing it down. These manipulations are achieved through the forms of language and presentation in which proposals and issues are couched and communicated.

Dutton also identifies similar tactics for modifying *issue sponsorship*. The *location* of an issue can be manipulated by attaching a powerful individual to it in some way, or by recruiting influential friends to its support. In the same way, *attachment* can be altered, through allowing more people to participate and to get involved to increase commitment. Finally, Dutton identifies tactics for modifying *agenda structure*, through changing the *size* or length of the current agenda (depending on what is realistic and manageable), and by changing the agenda *variety*, which can help to determine support for or resistance to new items. The *direction* of manipulation in each case will depend on the issue and on the context in which it is being introduced and pursued, and this is a matter of management judgement for the change agent.

Dutton argues that the agenda setting process is a conservative one, in which the issues that are most likely to attract attention tomorrow are those most similar to whatever attracted attention yesterday. This reinforces the bias towards incremental change identified by Quinn (1980). This conservatism can be defeated, Dutton argues, by new and influential executives who typically have an implicit mandate to change the agenda structure, and by the use of specific tactics which 'represent attempts to manage an issue's meaning for other organizational members' (Dutton, 1988, p. 138). These tactics can be effective, she argues, because the issues in hand often constitute ambiguous developments and events and are not concrete, at least in the initial stages, and the subjective impressions held by other organizational members can thus be more easily orchestrated.

Pettigrew does indicate the management actions which contribute to effective change implementation, based primarily on a four-phase model of the change process (lifted from an earlier source). One of the underlying concerns of this approach is with how changes acquire legitimacy and favour on the one hand, and with how proposals find disfavour on the other. A second underlying concern is with the timing of change – with the sequencing of events, the building of awareness and the establishment of consensus.

The four phases, which may overlap and which do not always necessarily occur in this sequence, involve:

1. Development of concern about the status quo.
2. Acknowledgement and understanding of the problem.
3. Planning and acting.
4. Stabilization.

In the initial 'problem sensing' stage, in which concern is aroused and developed in the organization, the role played by visionary leaders and 'early adopters' is critical. This stage is time consuming for those directly involved, and is often politically sensitive. The task of the change agent is to establish activities that 'educate the organization', and which broaden the support group. In the second 'acknowledgement' phase, in which the issue is widely recognized and accepted, the key management tasks are to keep talking and to sustain momentum. This again is likely to be time consuming, but the talking is often necessary to make sure that the support for and recognition of the problem are not deflected by other issues and priorities.

Pettigrew's characterization of planning and acting tasks is drawn from the organizational development literature (i.e. Beckhard and Harris, 1977). The advice offered includes, for example:

• Setting up management development initiatives which challenge existing thinking.
• Altering administrative mechanisms and career paths and reward systems.
• Forming task forces around issues and problems.
• Fragmenting a global vision into manageable bits.
• The exercise of patience, repetition and perseverance (which may involve waiting for individuals to leave or retire).
• Backing off and waiting until the time is right, for other reasons.
• Replacing those who leave – 'creative retirals' – with known supporters of the change proposals.
• Changing the organization structure and procedures.
• Promoting key individuals or 'role models' and changing their responsibilities at the same time.

These activities express Pettigrew's view of intervention in the organization's political and cultural systems, and of the symbolic activity involved in the management of meaning – building support, creating momentum, blocking resistance. These constitute deliberate actions to support and to perpetuate the required 'ideological reorientation'. There are similarities between this advice and Rosabeth Moss Kanter's advocacy of the use of 'power skills', 'team skills' and 'change architect skills' explained later in this chapter.

At the stabilization stage, the key management task is 'making things which happen stick', and this may again involve combinations of substantive and symbolic action such as adjusting rewards and information flows, and adjusting the distribution of power and authority in the organization to support new organizational arrangements. Tangible changes in communications, responsibilities and rewards are also symbolic in that they send signals to other members of the organization concerning management priorities and future intentions.

Pettigrew's four phases of change implementation are not on the surface significantly different from the project management life cycles discussed earlier, although the language is different. However, this characterization highlights aspects of these stages different from those in traditional linear models. Pettigrew also points out that this is an attempt to codify the stages and tasks involved in change without reducing the process to an over-determined and mechanical sequence of logical phases. Kanter (1983) describes the process of change in broadly similar terms, of three related waves of action, concerning problem definition and the collation of information, mobilizing a supportive coalition, and completion.

The key point here is that the practical implications of these perspectives are different from the project management emphasis on clear goals, roles, deadlines and budgets, and with the participative management advice about sympathetic involvement to ease acceptance and increase commitment.

We opened this chapter with a 'change formula' from David Gleicher of Arthur D. Little consultants. Capturing – and albeit simplifying – Andrew Pettigrew's perspective in a similar format produces the following:

Change will occur when $C \times V \times L > I$, where:

 C represents significant pressures and arguments for change in the inner and outer Context of the organization

 V represents the presence of Visionary leadership

 L represents the perceived Legitimacy of change proposals

 I represents the organizational Inertia sustained by the current dominant ideology

The strengths of Pettigrew's analysis are primarily theoretical and appear to derive from:

- The analytical location of strategic change processes and the change agent in the wider organizational and environmental context.
- Demonstrating how the rational and political are irrevocably intertwined.
- Highlighting the significance of legitimacy.

- The richness of the research agenda implied by this analytical frame, interrelating historical, contextual and processual issues.

The political realities of change and the central role of legitimacy are thus interestingly expressed, as are the varying influences of context and history in shaping the role of the change agent. This perspective also suggests the criteria that might be applied to establish the validity of explanations of change, concerning the multi-layered and multivariate nature of such explanations. Modes and issues for future investigation in this area are also addressed in an interesting and comprehensive way.

The weaknesses of Pettigrew's analysis, on the other hand, appear to derive from:

- The emphasis on the 'strategic' at the expense of other categories of organizational change.
- The richness and complexity of the perspective which disable attempts to derive parsimonious models of context and process.
- Minimal exploration of the interpersonal skills required to establish personal credibility and legitimacy for change proposals.
- The lack of practical advice about balancing the need to act in accordance with the custom and practice of the organization with 'behind the scenes' manipulations and interventions.

We are asked in this perspective to accept an intuitive definition of change as strategic, to put to one side as unimportant the control agenda of the project manager, and to work with a complex multivariate and multi-layer model of process and context which, while of considerable interest to the researcher, does not constitute a 'user friendly' guide to practical management action. The logics of problem solving and ownership are subordinated by a preoccupation with the logic of legitimacy. The social and interpersonal dynamics of the processes Pettigrew addresses are not explored in a manner that facilitates the easy identification of practical advice, and it is not clear how the 'intervention' skills he describes could be effectively developed. These criticisms should also be set in context; it was not Pettigrew's intention in the publications cited to develop and offer such detailed guidance.

The change agent's agendas

If the activities of leaders as strategic change agents are considered more exactly, then a whole series of these paradoxes emerge:

In strategy creation there is a need for vision yet detailed analysis.
In achieving credibility in an organization there is a need to be seen as insightful yet action oriented.

In questioning and challenging the status quo there is a need to maintain this credibility whilst attacking the existing paradigm.

In communicating strategic intent there is a need to encapsulate the complexity and vision of strategic thinking in mundane ways which have organizational meaning.

In achieving commitment to strategy there is a need to achieve focus of mission to overcome the ambiguity of a current situation likely to be in flux.

In consolidating a new strategy there is the need to maintain performance whilst breaking down old approaches and assumptions. (Johnson, 1990, p. 193)

The change agent typically faces a range of paradoxes and of apparently conflicting tasks, responsibilities and priorities. We have seen expressed in the previous section the potential need to manage the content, context and process of change simultaneously, and to act to establish legitimacy for change while conforming to accepted custom and practice in the culture of the organization. These conflicts are likely to be particularly acute in the organic, turbulent, high vulnerability contexts described in Chapter 2.

How can we express these conflicting priorities in a way that is of practical value to the change agent faced with such dilemmas? We also noted in Chapter 1 how the change agent has to deal with three parallel agendas. We noted in Chapter 2 that agenda priorities are contingent on context. Here we will be concerned primarily with the process agenda. The three agendas are as follows:

1. *The content agenda* It is widely accepted that you need a civil engineer as project manager for a construction project, and an information technology specialist for a management information system implementation. The project manager is expected to be technically competent and experienced with respect to the substance of the changes being implemented. Technical issues and problems are expected to arise and the project manager is expected to be qualified to deal with them – or to direct others in how to resolve the issues.

2. *The control agenda* Conventional project management texts and training courses concentrate on project control methodologies, such as critical path analysis and budgeting techniques. The project manager is thus expected to be familiar and competent with a range of planning, scheduling, budgeting, resourcing and monitoring techniques, with setting and meeting deadlines and targets. Problems with project monitoring and control are typically blamed in cases of delay or overspend. Project management training courses conventionally dwell on these issues to the exclusion of the other two agendas identified here.

3. *The process agenda* Sometimes covered under the heading of 'implementation skills', the project manager is expected to be competent in communications and consultation, in team building, in influencing and negotiating skills, and in the management of enthusiasm and resistance. The process agenda is thus

concerned with the broad range of human and organizational dimensions of change implementation. These skills are given different emphases in the different literatures of change management. Project management texts usually imply that the process agenda is subordinate to content and control agendas; sociological analyses emphasize process in general and, as we have seen, the need to establish legitimacy.

'Processual' models and explanations of change, particularly strategic change, suggest the relative importance of the process agenda. Study of the activity of change agents in practice could thus be expected to reinforce this view. In the perspective developed here, 'context' is not regarded as part of the agenda which the change agent is required to manage, but instead as the milieu in which the change agent functions, and which generates opportunities and constraints. In Pettigrew's perspective, the change agent is expected to manage context as well as content and process; instead, it is considered in our view as more helpful for the change agent to be aware of the nature of the context and of how this affects agenda priorities with respect to content, process and control. Context is thus to be seen, rather, as moulding, enabling, facilitating and constraining, rather than as a set of issues or parameters which the change agent has to manage.

What factors, in practice, influence the priority attached to the process agenda? An answer to this question was suggested towards the end of Chapter 2 where it was argued that the process agenda becomes increasingly important in organic contexts where the vulnerability of the change agent is high. It has been our experience in working with project managers that, in seminars, workshops and on training programmes, there is widespread willingness and readiness to accept the importance of the process agenda with respect to human and organizational factors in the successful management of change. However, it has frequently been pointed out to us in such settings that, once back in the organization, irrespective of organization type and nature of change, project managers push those human and organizational factors into the background, and focus on the 'foreground' issues of changes to procedure, of technology, of budgets and deadlines – in short, the content and control agendas. We have pursued this phenomenon with a number of management groups and the following possible explanations emerge for the inconsistency between what managers say outside their change projects, and what they do in practice. These concern:

- Goals: project goals are typically expressed in output and financial terms, and not in 'human' outcomes.
- Controls: project managers are typically rewarded for achieving quantifiable targets, not for keeping people happy.
- Roles: project management role definitions usually do not cover human or organizational issues in any significant depth.
- Intractability: project managers with technical qualifications and experience – content knowledge – often see the human or 'liveware' problems as intractable.

- Filling in: project managers can often afford to let some of the 'human relations' balls drop, as there are always people around willing to 'fill the gaps' and keep things working and moving.
- Comfort zones: project managers are often more comfortable working with the quantifiable, tangible and technical issues with which they are familiar, and find the 'soft' human and organizational dimensions are outside their personal zones of comfort.

The extent to which these explanations are valid in any particular setting has implications for the skills development of the individual project manager. There are, however, also organizational implications here for job descriptions, and for the appraisal and reward of project managers. Approaches to the development of change agent competences are examined in Chapter 5. It is useful to point out here, however, that such development must take into account organizational factors as well as individual attributes.

From the survey mentioned in Chapter 1, the rank ordering of those explanations in the experience of respondents was as follows, with that ranked first being seen to apply most often:

1. The way in which goals were expressed.
2. The way in which roles were defined.
3. Time pressure to achieve targets.
4. Human issues outside comfort zones.
5. Perceived intractability of people problems.
6. People 'filling in' when problems arose.

This ranking suggests that preoccupation with the control agenda displaces concern for process. A separate section of the survey questionnaire asked respondents to rate a series of thirty explanations for 'why projects go wrong'. The twelve most popular reasons were:

1. Top managers not providing enough support and commitment.
2. Objectives of the change not clearly identified.
3. Line or function managers not being sufficiently involved in the project.
4. Responsibilities for tasks not clearly defined and allocated to individuals.
5. Problems and changes ignored until too late.
6. Progress monitored in a haphazard way.
7. Corrective actions delayed or ignored.
8. The project group never really worked as a team.
9. Inadequate time and effort invested in planning.
10. Some key people who could make or break the project were left out of discussions.
11. Department or sectional interests took precedence over organizational needs.
12. Project leaders lacked the right mix of technical, business and interpersonal skills.

These problem factors reflect an equal mix of control (2, 4, 5, 6, 7, 9) and process (1, 3, 8, 10, 11, 12) agenda concerns. In contrast, the six problems rated as least important in the experience of the respondents to this survey included 'not enough staff allocated to the job', 'impatience for results leading to short cuts', 'unexpected problems or changes being allowed to disrupt the project', 'unrealistic expectations leading to rapid disillusionment when problems appeared', 'losing key personnel', and 'keeping the project compartmentalized'.

We also argued in Chapter 2 that agenda priorities are influenced by the vulnerability of the change agent in different contexts. It was suggested that, in a low vulnerability context, the content and control agendas take priority, and that there may be minimal risk involved in ignoring the process agenda. In a high vulnerability context, on the other hand, it was argued that the process agenda must take priority and that, while the control agenda remains important, the content agenda has a relatively lower priority for the change agent. This characterization of the agenda priorities in a high vulnerability context threatens the conventional wisdom that the project manager should always have content expertise.

What are the skills required to deal with the process agenda? Attention has focused recently on the need for project managers in highly technical areas, such as information systems applications, to have strengths in interpersonal and social skills. Some commentators have even suggested that interpersonal competence can be more important than technical understanding for the project manager. Ring (1989, p. 28), for example, reporting on a survey of 191 management information system professionals carried out by the Andersen Consulting firm, claims that: 'The most important element was to have a good project manager with good interpersonal skills.' The selection of a good 'technician' was often regarded as a problem. Ring concludes that the effective project manager has to be an 'all-rounder', with competence in team building, staff motivation, empowering others, giving others responsibility, credit and independence, giving feedback, listening, picking up problems quickly, taking criticism, and accepting responsibility. Ring (1989, p. 29) quotes one manager as commenting: 'I doubt whether the average IT person has a wide enough breadth of vision to do this. If you're looking for project leaders, I think it's easier to teach a little bit of IT to a businessman than it is to teach business to IT people.'

We will explore further recent research in this area in Chapter 4, and will here concentrate on what a number of commentators have identified as the 'political' or 'power' skills of the change agent, which go significantly beyond the exercise of interpersonal skills.

'Power skills' and the change agent

Following the contention that the change process is rarely rational and linear in reality, a number of commentators have offered practical advice on the management conduct required to operate in what is generally described as the 'political' domain of the organization.

Tom Burns (1961) in his discussion of the micropolitics of institutional change clearly establishes the concepts of organizations as political systems, and of politics as a mode of behaviour concerned with the pursuit of individual and group self-interests. In Burns's (1961, p. 278) definition, 'politics are the exploitation of resources, both physical and human, for the achievement of more control over others, and thus of safer, or more comfortable, or more satisfying terms of individual existence.' These are widely accepted and largely uncontentious statements about organizational behaviour. However, Burns makes some additional observations about the nature of political behaviour in organizations, particularly in the light of our earlier discussion of the tension between the public and backstage activity of the change agent, and in the context of Pettigrew's arguments concerning the process of change as the 'management of meaning'.

Burns' first main point of interest to our discussion, concerning another widely accepted notion, relates to the central role of political action in generating social and organizational change. Large and complex organizations have widened the scope for political action through the consequent accumulation of physical and human resources. From the perspective of the individual in the organization, there is both more to play with, and more to play for.

Burns' second point of interest to our discussion concerns the way in which political behaviour in the organization is invariably concealed, regulated and rendered acceptable by subtle shifts in the language in which action is described:

> Normally, either side in any conflict called political by observers claims to speak in the interests of the corporation as a whole. In fact, the only recognized, indeed feasible, way of advancing political interests is to present them in terms of improved welfare or efficiency, as contributing to the organization's capacity to meet its task and to prosper. In managerial and academic, as in other legislatures, both sides to any debate claim to speak in the interests of the community as a whole; this is the only permissible mode of expression.
>
> It is backstage, so to speak, that the imputations of empire-building, caucus log-rolling, squaring, and obstructionism occur. The linguistic division, which is also a moral one, is particularly marked in universities, where mutually exclusive sets of expressions exist for discussion in faculty meetings or committees, and in bars, common rooms, or parties. (Burns, 1961, p. 260)

The change agent is thus advised to pay attention to language and setting. Can I speak in this way to this group in this situation? It is legitimate, for example, to seek to damage perceptions of the competence and credibility of other individuals and groups in what Burns labels 'gossip sessions'. In formal meetings, such discussion is proscribed because the author of such statements will attract public suspicion of being in pursuit of personal gain. The change agent is thus advised to pay attention to what will be regarded as 'acceptable argument' in a given setting.

Burns also points out that personal motives are acknowledged in organizational action, and are indeed recognized as valuable as expressions of drive, ambition, enterprise and initiative. Personal motives contribute to career success and are thus legitimately pursued. So, 'while there is a dual linguistic and moral code attached to the co-operative and competitive aspects of society and its constituent systems, there is also a sense in which we recognize both kinds of value, incompatible as they may appear to be in the discussion of immediate issues concerning the distribution of rewards and resources' (Burns, 1961, p. 262).

Despite earlier remarks about the language in which these actions are publicly articulated, the simultaneous pursuit of organizational goals and personal ambition is therefore regarded as acceptable and 'legitimate'. The change agent is thus advised to proceed with this in mind, but to be sensitive to the social context in which actions are exposed for scrutiny. Burns describes how a senior laboratory manager could explain to his colleagues how he removed documents from another department to help in preparing an estimate for an important contract, knowing that his colleagues would approve of and praise such action. The same explanation offered to the manager of that other department would doubtless have a different reception. This kind of backstage activity is thus rendered legitimate by appeal to the wider interests of the organization and to the sectional interests of groups within it.

Morley (1990) offers similar advice to the data processing (DP) manager seeking to convince a board of directors of the value of proposed investments in new systems. As the board is usually impressed only by demonstrations of cost effectiveness, skills in 'selling up' are required, in order to manipulate board members' perceptions and decisions: 'Today's DP manager must plot the presentation to the board with as much cunning as he or she would devote to bargaining with IT suppliers.' Morley describes new systems development at Girobank, arguing that quantitative and qualitative cost benefit analysis is important, but also arguing for the necessity of 'an arsenal of points', and:

> Planning for the sell to the board also entailed putting the personality of individual directors under scrutiny. We gained a view of the personality, disposition and potential hostility of various directors and decided that it would be in our best interests to keep the presentation as short as possible. (Morley, 1990, p. 21)

In the event, the new managing director had to leave the presentation halfway through, and the presentation failed. It took another meeting with a 'low-tech' summary of what was involved and the support of representatives from another company that had successfully introduced the same system to swing the decision in the DP manager's favour.

Rosabeth Moss Kanter (1983) identifies what she calls 'change architect skills' for the change agent, which include effective articulation or definition of proposals for change. The standard project management advice is, define your project, your problem and your goal clearly. That is easier to say than it is to achieve in practice. There are some clear definitions that are better and more effective than others, particularly when it comes to winning ready support, and anticipating resistance. Kanter suggests that there are at least seven attributes of a 'good' project definition. These are attributes that increase the acceptability of what is being proposed. She suggests that, where possible, a proposal for change should be presented in terms that make it sound, for example:

- Trial-able: it should appear capable of being subjected to a pilot before going the whole way down the track with the scheme and with all its effort and expense.
- Reversible: convince your audience that what you are proposing can be changed back to today's status quo if it falls to pieces.
- Divisible: where your project has a number of separate dimensions, present these as potentially independent aspects of a broader change programme – so when single issues cause problems the whole package doesn't have to fold.
- Concrete: make the changes and their outcomes tangible and avoid expressing what will happen in abstract and general terms which do not convey an accurate feel for the proposals.
- Familiar: make proposals in terms that other people in the organization can recognize and feel familiar with, because if what you propose is so far over the horizon that people don't recognize it, they'll feel out of their comfort zones and start resisting.
- Congruent: proposals for change should where possible be seen to 'fit' within the rest of the organization and be consistent with existing policy and practice – or at least consistent with other parallel changes.
- Sexy: choose projects that have publicity value – whether in terms of external or media relations, or in terms of the internal politics of the organization; what will the local press latch on to, and what will the chief executive get excited about?

Clearly it is not possible always to define every set of change proposals unequivocally in such terms. However, all that Kanter is suggesting is that, where it is possible and appropriate, proposals worded in such a way that they appear to possess more of these attributes are more likely to meet acceptance. We are here not dealing directly with deceit, but with the careful manipulation of the language of change proposals, in a covert attempt to increase acceptability and to deflect counter-argument and resistance.

British Telecom, in the in-house project management handbook mentioned in

Chapter 1, offers similar advice on the wording of project proposals, suggesting that certain terms should be avoided, such as:

- discover
- devise
- define
- review
- revise

These words should not be used in project proposals because, the manual states, they imply preliminary analysis, delay and procrastination. This language suggests to readers that the analysis, which should have been completed before the proposals were made public, has still to be carried out. The implied need for further study suggests that the problem is not well understood and that there is going to be delay. Proposals worded in that way are thus less likely to be accepted than proposals that include such terms as:

- reduce
- remove
- eliminate
- meet target
- improve
- maintain
- do

These terms, on the other hand, imply understanding, action and progress. This language leads readers to assume that the problem is already well understood and that positive steps are being taken to address it – now. This section of the change agent's manual concludes:

> Just using the 'right' words to formulate your proposals can have an impact on the ease with which a project gets off the ground and on the chances of managing it to a successful conclusion.

This advice again suggests covert manipulation of the publicity given to proposals for change within the organization. This is a further dimension of what Pettigrew (1985) calls 'the management of meaning' in the change process. What is being managed here is, rather, people's perceptions of the meaning of change proposals.

Kanter and Pettigrew are not alone in this view of the manipulative role of the change agent. Peter Keen (1981), for example, offers interesting advice on how to block technical and organizational change, and how to counter such blocking manoeuvres. He describes these methods in terms of the organizational politics of counter-implementation and counter-counter-implementation strategies respectively. His prescription is aimed at change agents dealing with applications of management information systems, but it is a simple matter to translate this advice into other organizational change settings.

Keen offers the following advice on counter-implementation strategies:

- *Divert resources* Split the budget across other projects; have key staff given other priorities and allocate them to other assignments; arrange for equipment to be moved or shared.
- *Exploit intertia* Suggest that everyone wait until a key player has taken action, or read the report, or made an appropriate response; suggest that the results from some other project should be monitored and assessed first.
- *Keep goals vague and complex* It is harder to initiate appropriate action in pursuit of aims that are multi-dimensional and that are specified in generalized, grandiose or abstract terms.
- *Encourage and exploit lack of organizational awareness* Insist that 'we can deal with the people issues later', knowing that these will delay or kill the project.
- *'Great idea – let's do it properly'* And let's bring in representatives from this function and that section, until we have so many different views and conflicting interests that it will take forever to sort them out.
- *Dissipate energies* Have people conduct surveys, collect data, prepare analyses, write reports, make overseas trips, hold special meetings . . .
- *Reduce the champion's influence and credibility* Spread damaging rumours, particularly among the champion's friends and supporters.
- *Keep a low profile* It is not effective openly to declare resistance to change because that gives those driving change a clear target to aim for.

This advice is clearly helpful to the change agent in two respects. First, in attempts to block changes promoted by others in the organization. Second, to recognize counter-implementation strategies being used to block the change in hand. Counter-implementation is not always easily recognized, and in this respect, the last point on Peter Keen's list of strategies is the most significant. It is not necessary in attempting to block change publicly to declare resistance. On the contrary, some counter-implementation behaviour is covert, and it may be just as effective, or more effective, openly to support change by using, for example, the 'let's do it properly' approach.

What does the change agent do when confronted by the use of counter-implementation strategies of this kind? Keen offers the following advice on counter-counter-implementation strategies (which are, in effect, basic implementation tools):

- *Establish clear direction and objectives* Goal clarity enables action to proceed more effectively than ambiguity and complexity which can slow down action.
- *Establish simple, phased programming* For the same reasons as having clear goals.
- *Adopt a fixer – facilitator – negotiator role* Resistance to change can rarely be overcome by reason alone and the exercise of these interpersonal skills is required.

- *Seek and respond to resistance* See Kanter's techniques for blocking interference below – it can be more effective to take a proactive approach to resistance in order to overcome, mitigate or block it.
- *Rely on face to face* See Keen's earlier point about the fixer role – personal influence and persuasion are usually more effective in winning and sustaining support than the impersonal memo or report.
- *Create a prior 'felt need'* If people want change because they have had the reasons explained to them, then resistance is likely to be minimal.
- *Build personal credibility* By sustaining a professional image and integrity, by displaying expertise and credibility.
- *Coopt support early* Kanter speaks of coalition building, and of recruiting backers, as of prior importance in comparison with team building.
- *Exploit a crisis, which may be part of creating the felt need* People will often respond more positively to a crisis which they understand and face collectively than to personal attempts to change their behaviour.
- *The meaningful steering committee; or task force or project team* It should include in its membership key players in the organization who carry 'weight', and authority and respect.

Once again, we are dealing in large part here with covert action, rather than with public behaviour, designed to sidestep as well as to overcome resistance and to stimulate support through means other than straightforward reasoning and argument. It is, however, interesting to note that Keen's first two and last counter-counter-implementation strategies are wholly consistent with much conventional project management advice.

Kanter (1983) offers broadly similar advice on what she calls the 'power skills' of the change agent, under the heading of 'techniques for blocking interference'. These techniques include:

- Wait them out: in time, they should eventually go away if you persist.
- Wear them down: keep pushing, keep arguing, and again your persistence should eventually prevail.
- Appeal to higher authority: which can either be senior management (you better agree because the boss does), or to a set of values or standards (such as standards of health care in a hospital – which have to be maintained).
- Invite them in: have them join the party, coopt them onto the steering group.
- Send emissaries: ask friends, in whom you know your resistors believe, to talk to them and convince them.
- Display support: make sure that your people are present and vocal at key meetings.
- Reduce the stakes: make changes where possible in areas that are

particularly damaging to key individuals and groups.

* Warn them off: let them know that senior management, and perhaps other key actors, will challenge their dissent.

Chris Argyris (1988), describing management strategies for handling the potential conflict between control and autonomy in decentralized organization structures, advocates the use of what he calls 'the mixed message'. This means, tell them that they have the authority, that it is their show, but make sure that you provide helpful intervention. This is achieved through providing messages that are both clear and ambiguous, precise and imprecise. As an example, the message, 'you are running this show', can be combined with the signal, 'we require a corporate perspective'. Argyris offers four rules for achieving this. Design an inconsistent message, act as if the message is not inconsistent, make the inconsistency undiscussable, and 'make the undiscussability of the undiscussable also undiscussable' (Argyris, 1988, p. 346). As a brief illustration, he cites the following experience:

> The executive took the actions described above [concerning an application of the 'mixed message' technique] and covered up the reasons that underlay them. I make this inference because it would be difficult for the strategy to work if, for example, the executive stated openly to the subordinates that his actions were designed to reduce their resistance and power. (Argyris, 1988, p. 348)

From their research into 'strategic redirection' in sixteen American and European multinational companies, Doz and Prahalad (1988) offer a four-stage model of the change process similar to that of Pettigrew. The four stages in this account concern 'incubation', 'variety generation', 'power shifts' and 'refocusing'. They argue that effective 'incubation' requires a senior manager with a vision which cuts against the 'accepted strategic logic' and who is able to articulate that vision and elicit commitment to it. The 'variety generation' stage involves further undermining of 'the legitimacy of the prevalent conventional wisdom' through a number of channels. This can include the creation of a sense of impending crisis, and emphasizing competitive weaknesses. This also involves broadening the discussion of organizational issues through offering a wider choice of options, and through outlining extreme options – to prompt rejection in favour of the change agent's solution.

The third phase in this model involves 'power shifts' which are in effect a series of minor reallocations of authority. Doz and Prahalad argue that this can involve no formal changes to organization structure, but rather apparently minor and beneficial changes 'that could not easily be opposed by any of the executives concerned' (1988, p. 74). In the fourth phase, 'refocusing', the legitimacy of the strategic redirection is reinforced by changes to formal management systems, by key management moves and appointments, and by other changes to information flows and resources to allow the change to be permanently anchored.

In these attempts to alter the 'cognitive perspective' of the organization's members, Doz and Prahalad identify the tools of the change agent in three categories, concerning data management tools, managers' management tools, and conflict management tools:

1. *Data management tools* These concern the manipulation of information systems, resource allocation procedures, strategic planning and budgeting arrangements. These tools 'provide and structure the data pertinent to the critical strategic decision and to the global and local performance of the company. By structuring such data and focusing the attention of executives on specific aspects, these tools transform raw data into useful information for decision-making and strategic control' (Doz and Prahalad, 1988, p. 76).
2. *Managers' management tools* This involves a combination of 'hard' and 'soft' approaches. The 'hard' tools include manipulation of key appointments, career planning and reward systems. The 'soft' tools include changes to management development and socialization patterns. These tools 'shape executives' perceptions of self-interest and of their expectations by defining "rules of the game" within the firm. Promotion and appointment processes, individual evaluations, rewards and punishment and management development processes, for instance, all help to communicate rules of the game to the various senior and middle-level executives within the firm' (Doz and Prahalad, 1988, p. 76).
3. *Conflict management tools* This involves reallocation of decision responsibility, formation of business teams, task forces, and coordination committees, the appointment of 'integrators', and the establishment of procedures to resolve issues. These tools, 'provide channels and structures for contentious decisions to be made, in particular decisions which require critical trade-offs' (Doz and Prahalad, 1988, p. 76).

Doz and Prahalad argue that data management is useful during the early refinement of strategic priorities. Manager management is helpful in unlocking and challenging dominant perspectives; 'soft' approaches achieve this during the early stages of change and 'hard' tools can then be used to make power shifts visible and stable. Conflict resolution tools are useful in later stages of change to establish new perspectives and to help make necessary power reallocations.

Doz and Prahalad thus seek to offer advice to the change agent for effectively altering the perceptions of the organization's members with respect to change, through the manipulation of appointments, structures, information and reward systems, task forces and other problem-solving groups, and through management development initiatives. This account has clear similarities with that of Pettigrew (1985; 1987), with specific advice attached to each stage of the change implementation process. While these authors are concerned with strategic change and strategic redirection, the stages in the change process and the tools identified can be appropriate in other change settings. However, neither Doz and Prahalad nor Pettigrew emphasize the difficulties facing the change agent in 'playing' with the wheels and levers of the organization in the manner described to achieve the desired end results. Change agents do not always have easy and direct access to decisions affecting structures, appointments and systems. Doz and Prahalad in particular appear to write with the chief executive in mind, and not for other middle or senior managers who can also often find themselves implementing changes with similar problems. The change agent who does not have instant access to the domain of senior management decision and control may thus be required to rely more heavily on 'backstage' activity to sustain the momentum of the change implementation process.

Manipulation and threat as change management techniques

How, we asked in Chapter 1, should the change agent proceed when the advice on offer is impractical and unrealistic? We noted in that while the easy prescription from the literatures of project management and participative management may be appropriate in some settings, the change agent may not always have the time, the expertise, the resources or the clear priorities to follow that advice in textbook style. We also noted, however, that the literatures of project management and participative management advised against the use of manipulation and threat as appropriate tools for the organizational change agent. Are we dismissing these tools too quickly, and do they offer effective alternatives to or complements to conventional change management advice?

If we accept Pettigrew's arguments about the need to establish legitimacy for change, and about change as the management of meaning, it is difficult to see how change can proceed effortlessly without the exercise of counter-counter-implementation strategies, without appropriately worded change definition, without the exercise of power skills, without symbolic actions to focus attention and reinforce decisions. The advice of Dutton, Kanter, Keen, Johnson, and of Doz and Prahalad appears highly relevant in this respect too, particularly with 'quadrant four' changes in fuzzy organizational settings where the vulnerability of the change agent is high. Part of the answer to our question about the impracticality of traditional advice thus concerns the advocacy of some relatively unconventional techniques, in the domain of manipulation and threat. This raises definitional issues concerning what precisely is meant by these terms in practice.

Manipulation takes a number of different forms. Some of the manipulation identified in this chapter has concerned the creative and appropriate use of language. This can affect the way in which change proposals are presented and justified, and also which proposals are presented, and in what format. We have identified tactics that can be deployed to orchestrate the impressions held by an organization's members concerning the salience and sponsorship of particular issues and their place on the management agenda. We have seen how the language of definition can be used to broaden the boundaries of debate, to hasten or retard the introduction of change, and how it can overcome or create resistance by colouring perceptions of what is being proposed. We have also suggested that the language in which change and its promoters and resistors can be discussed will differ across different social contexts in the organization. The change agent is thus advised to pay careful attention to the style of presentations and reports in which change proposals are advanced and discussed.

We have also seen how organizational systems can be manipulated to highlight and prioritize specific issues and to encourage or discourage particular behaviours. Information, reward and promotion systems are obvious choices here. The introduction of new management development programmes, new administrative procedures, and new steering committees or task forces can play a similar role. We have also suggested that the organization structure itself can be manipulated to direct attention and channel energies in particular directions. And individuals may be subject to manipulation also, through placing key supporters in key roles, through waiting until particular individuals leave the organization, and through 'creative retirals' which open the way for others.

The management advice derived from these models of process also concerns the manipulation of face-to-face relationships, in establishing friendships and support, in the formation of teams or task forces, in selling ideas, in attempting to block interference, and in negotiating. It is thus being suggested here that personal relationships should be exploited and manipulated in the interests of change implementation.

Threat also takes a number of different forms. This may be wholly implicit, through the delay or withdrawal, for example, of reward, promotion or other forms of career enhancement (such as attachment to prestigious project teams) in order to foster and encourage wider agreement and commitment to specific proposals for change. The potential loss to some individuals or groups faced with change can often be mitigated – or by implication exacerbated – through action by the change agent. The implied threat of being 'frozen out' of future developments and plans can be a significant inducement to support current proposals. We have also seen how appeal to the positive views of more senior management can be held against less senior managers who are thinking of offering to block change proposals.

This argument potentially raises ethical as well as terminological issues; manipulation and threat are generally regarded as unprofessional and immoral actions to take in any context. The theoretical argument developed here, if applied inappropriately in practice, could clearly have a devastating effect on the change attempt, and on the change agent. There are, however, a number of dimensions to the response to those who would for ethical reasons wish to reject out of hand the advice offered by this argument.

First, there is Burns' point about the dual moral and linguistic codes pertaining to individual and organizational goals. Given the particular manner in which 'appropriate manipulation and threat' have been identified here, most of us regard such behaviour as acceptable and ethical – in context. We must recall here Burns' point about the *relativity* of perceptions of dishonest or unethical behaviour; such acts which are seen to promote 'our' common good may not always be seen as acceptable to 'them' elsewhere in the organization. Notions of what is ethical or not are thus relative and contextual, and are not absolute.

Burns' argument about dual moral and linguistic codes is echoed in the distinction made by March and Olson (1983) between what they call the rhetoric of administration and the rhetoric of realpolitik in the context of major change in public administration. The rhetoric of orthodox administrative theory, they argue:

> speaks of the design of administrative structures and procedures to facilitate the efficiency and effectiveness of bureaucratic hierarchies . . . proclaims that explicit, comprehensive planning of administrative structures is necessary, that piecemeal change creates chaos . . . emphasizes economy and control . . . speaks of offices that could be abolished, salaries that could be reduced, positions that could be eliminated, and expenses that could be curtailed. (March and Olson, 1983, pp. 282–3)

The contrasting rhetoric of realpolitik, they argue:

> speaks of reorganization . . . in terms of a political struggle among contending interests. Fundamental political interests, within the bureaucracy and outside, seek access, representation, control, and policy benefits . . . organizational forms reflect victorious interests and establish a mechanism for future dominance . . . the design of an administrative structure is an important political issue, to be effective the reorganization process must reflect the heterogeneous milieu and the values, beliefs, and interests present in ordinary legislative processes. (March and Olson, 1983, p. 283)

Thus while administrative orthodoxy emphasizes management control, the realpolitik perspective prescribes attention to political control. They do not argue that an older administrative rhetoric has been replaced by a modern realization underpinned by realpolitik. They do not argue that these perspectives are competing for legitimacy. They argue instead that these two rhetorics consistently run through historical analyses and contemporary commentary on reorganization:

> Such a perspective may provide an interpretation of the cultural ritual of reorganization and of the rhetorical duality of that ritual. The rhetoric of administration and the rhetoric of realpolitik are mutually supporting and are embedded in a culture in which each is important. The ritual of reorganization is a reminder of both sets of beliefs and a testimony to their efficacy. On the one hand, a commitment to administrative purity is made tolerable by an appreciation of realpolitik, much as a commitment to personal purity is made

tolerable by an appreciation of human weakness. At the same time, a commitment to realpolitik rhetoric is made consistent with human hopes by a faith in the imaginability of improvement through human intelligence. It should not be surprising to find that both rhetorics survive and thrive, and that both find expression in the symbols of reorganization. The orthodoxy of administration is the voice of the prologue to comprehensive administrative reform; the orthodoxy of realpolitik is the voice of the epilogue; the myths of the first shade into the myths of the second over the course of a major effort at reorganization; and both sets of myths are needed for a normatively proper interpretation of the reorganization saga. (March and Olson, 1983, p. 291)

Although March and Olson write about major administrative reform in the institutions of American government, their argument can be related to the perspectives introduced in Chapter 3 concerning the role of ritual and of symbolic action in the management of organizational change. Arguments for and against the ethical propriety of manipulation and threat, in the ways in which these terms have been discussed here, become less symmetrical if we accept the duality of moral and linguistic codes, the duality of perspective on reorganization, and a duality in social beliefs. In contrast, in arguing that 'reorganization is a domain of rhetoric, trading, problematic attention, and symbolic action', March and Olson (1983, p. 291) appear to suggest that the tensions between and intertwinings of these two rhetorics supply the motives, the creativity and the dynamism behind attempts at organizational change. Questions of ethical validity rather concern what is acceptable, what is appropriate, what is anticipated, and what is seen as necessary to pursue a particular line of action in a given context. We thus return to situational ethics, rather than to a universal view of what constitutes ethically appropriate behaviour.

Second, from a more pragmatic perspective, it would be foolish for us to proceed with the assumption that other organizational actors conscientiously avoid 'counter-implementation' techniques, conscientiously avoid the careful wording of proposals, or conscientiously avoid the exercise of 'power skills' in the pursuit either of personal or organizational gain. This is not just a 'tit for tat' argument, but rather the basis of a case for rendering such behaviour open to observation and to discussion, and to conscious rather than unconscious control.

Third, in the way that dental and medical intervention can be both painful and benign in the interests of the patient, manipulation and threat as described here in the pursuit of desirable organizational change can also be considered as 'benign intervention'. This of course assumes that the changes proposed are indeed being introduced in the best long-term interests of the organization and its members.

Finally, Child (1984, p. 285) argues that, while a participative approach to organizational change may be 'ethically the correct procedure', it is necessary to confront issues of organizational politics and not avoid them. He argues that 'whatever the ethical and ideological attractions of participation, there are only some situations in which it is likely to succeed as a means of implementing organizational change' (Child, 1984, p. 291). The organizational conditions which favour participation, Child argues, include the following:

- No definite time-limit; lack of urgency; survival of the organization is not at stake.
- Participants' help is required to design change, and commitment is required to make it work.
- Need for change is not widely or clearly recognized.
- Participants expect to be involved, as an aspect of the established procedure or culture.
- Some resistance is anticipated, but not a challenge to underlying objectives.
- The power of the promoter is limited, but is not wholly constrained.

Where different conditions prevail, Child argues, participative or consultative approaches to change implementation are likely to fail, and the change agent has to resort to other approaches. Participation is clearly a waste of time, he points out, where either there is total agreement to the changes, or where management has power to force through a preferred solution. A participative approach will equally be ineffective where the opposition is inflexible, or where there is fundamental disagreement – and where participation will simply create opportunities for obstruction and delay. This analysis seems to advocate the deployment of political or 'power' skills on the part of the change agent where appropriate, given the above considerations.

   None of this is to deny that the methods and techniques described here have no moral or ethical problems. We have presented these issues in part as something of a 'language game' – a semantic contest in which those who can most effectively orchestrate the impressions of others through clever communication and dialogue will win support for their perspective. The reality of organizational power, however, means that change is also a 'power game' in which some individuals and groups have greater access to the resources that facilitate such manipulation than others. The unscrupulous use of such manipulative approaches is of course potentially highly damaging to those who happen to be on the receiving end. However, we wish to defend the position that this is not necessarily the case, and that these approaches are, in context, justifiable and legitimate intervention techniques that are indispensable to the change agent.

   It is necessary also not to overemphasize this aspect of the role of the change agent. This chapter has been concerned with models of the process of change that offer perspectives different from those derived from project or participative management. Pettigrew's perspective takes us directly to such political and social process issues through a model of change which highlights 'the management of meaning', in which 'legitimacy' plays a central role, and in which the key competences of the change agent involve 'intervening in the political and cultural systems of the organization'. We are thus in danger of losing sight of the content and control agendas of the change agent through this preoccupation with process. As argued earlier, this preoccupation is partly correct when the change agent is working in quadrant four and in an organic, turbulent organizational context. Even in a 'high vulnerability' context, the control agenda retains importance and, although perhaps secondary, cannot be overlooked or avoided.

In Chapter 4 we will return to explorations of the competences of the change agent or project manager which do not force attention so exclusively on to political and social process skills. We have seen in this chapter how the process of change can be seen as multi-layered and multi-dimensional, with some activity public, and some backstage. The rational-linear model can be seen as a ritualized, anticipated, and organizationally expected approach which serves to legitimate the change proposals and the change agent in the perceptions of the organizational public. The logic of problem solving, represented in project management manuals, is typically a logic that has to be seen in most organizations to unfold in an acceptable manner. This is an attribute of the rational-linear model which Pettigrew tends to overlook. As a guide to the expected public performance of the change agent, these apparently oversimplified linear models should not be dismissed. However, it seems that, in high vulnerability contexts, the change agent is required to exercise other skills in the prosecution of proposals, and these are not necessarily behaviours acceptable at the level of public discussion or internal report. Wearing people down and buying them off to block resistance are not commonly regarded as acceptable items of conversation and discussion. We have argued here, however, that these are nevertheless acceptable and legitimate forms of backstage action for the change agent.

The expertise of the change agent cannot, therefore, be expressed and understood independently of an understanding of the process of change and the context in which it is undertaken. One feature of the 'management competences' debate of the late 1980s in Britain was the generation of what are thought to be relevant lists of competences which can be learned, developed and assessed singly. That debate paid little attention to the context in which such competences would be deployed. What we shall seek to establish in the following chapter is that the competences of the change agent are relatively straightforward, and relatively well understood, where competences are defined singly and simply.

We shall also argue, however, that the possession of these competences does not render any manager an effective change agent. What is equally important is the ability appropriately to deploy those competences in context. The expertise of the change agent is thus seen to be characterized by the diagnostic and judgemental capabilities necessary to achieve the appropriate deployment of acquired competences in particular organizational and change contexts. The diagnostic and judgemental capabilities highlighted in this chapter thus concern the extent to which the change agent is required to resort to the use of power skills, to manipulation and threat, to counter-counter-implementation strategies, and to other forms of backstage activity – and the precise nature and timing of that activity – in support of the organizationally required public performance.

4

A model of expertise

The argument so far

What then are the key competences of the change agent to be derived from the preceding analysis? How does the reality of change management compare with the theory? Let us first summarize the argument so far.

In Chapter 1, we discussed the potentially conflicting advice available to the change agent, from the project management, participative management and sociological literatures. By looking at the processes of change from different perspectives, these accounts offer different models of the implementation process and thus emphasize different dimensions of change management expertise. We identified the different 'unfolding logics' in these three perspectives, concerning the logic of problem solving, the logic of establishing ownership, and the logic of establishing legitimacy respectively. We also identified the three main agendas of the change agent. The project management literature emphasizes the content and control agendas. The participative management literature emphasizes the social processes central to effective change. The sociological literature also emphasizes the process agenda, but concentrates on political and cultural issues, on context, and on the need to manage the perceptions of organizational members through ritual and symbolic action.

In Chapter 2 we discussed how the 'vulnerability' of the change agent is increased through the development of organic organizational forms, and through the migration of change to quadrant four which concerns radical change affecting the core of the business. It was also pointed out that, through such organizational developments, the activity of many middle and senior managers had become more change- and project-oriented, and that the apparently specialized skills of the project manager may now apply to general management also. We established that the context in quadrant four is often characterized by frequent shifts in goals and priorities, by tight organizational interdependencies, by conflicts about responsibility for change and its outcomes, and by potential uncertainty with respect to the views of senior management. We also argued that, in a high vulnerability context, the change agent is advised to concentrate on the process and control agendas, in that order of priority, and to delegate the content agenda to other members of the project team. The social, cultural and political dimensions of the change process thus assume higher importance for the change agent in a high vulnerability context.

In Chapter 3 we examined models of the process of change emphasizing social and political aspects and identifying the implications of these perspectives for the change agent. This portrayed the change agent as manipulative and devious, sustaining the 'public performance' of proposing and justifying change with 'backstage activity' in framing discussion in appropriate terms and establishing adequate support among other organizational members. This provides an account of the social and interpersonal skills required by the change agent different from that which is typically offered in the participative management and organizational development literature. The open, public, social processes of involvement in change are thus complemented by the backstage, political, manipulative activities in shaping perceptions of change.

In this chapter we will report the results of research which sought to establish a competence-based view of the attributes of the effective change agent. The analysis is based on the audio diary study explained earlier. The competences identified here are thus derived from the first-hand accounts of the practical experiences of change agents working through recent or current change management activities. Having identified the competences from the audio diary analysis, we will then illustrate them briefly from selected diary entries, in the words of the managers themselves.

These competences turn out to be relatively well understood, although the question of how they can best be developed remains open. However, the mere possession of these competences alone is inadequate and, as argued at the end of Chapter 3, it is the ability to deploy those separately identified competences appropriately in context which really counts as change management expertise. It is important not to lose sight of the fact that the individual competences identified here are relatively straightforward. As we have seen, some of the sociological accounts of change processes have offered rich theoretical insights while potentially mystifying the process from a practical management point of view. We will thus draw a distinction between 'tools for analysis' and 'tools for action', and concentrate on the latter in concluding this chapter with a model of competence for the contemporary change agent.

Fifteen competences

The concept of competence applied to the management task in general or to change management in particular has some instant intuitive appeal. If the competences can be established, management selection, training and development, and performance assessment become straightforward matters. A Training Commission Advisory Group on the classification of management competences defined the term as:

the ability to perform the activities within an occupation. Competence is a

wide concept which embodies the ability to transfer skills and knowledge to
new situations within the occupational area. It encompasses organization and
planning of work, innovation and coping with non-routine activities. It
includes those qualities of personal effectiveness that are required in the
workplace to deal with co-workers, managers and customers. (Training
Commission, 1988, p. 14)

This definition offers an all-encompassing notion of competence. The task, as the
Training Commission and subsequent commentators working with the same
perspective see it, is to find an appropriate mode for the meaningful classification
of competences, as the basis of a scheme of assessment and national vocational
management qualifications. The term is also now used to refer to specific units and
elements of individual ability. The Training Commission report continues:

An element of competence describes what can be done; an action, behaviour
or outcome which a person should be able to demonstrate. Or an element of
competence may describe such things as the knowledge or understanding
which is essential if performance is to be sustained, or extended to new
situations within the occupation. Each element of competence has associated
performance criteria which define the expected level of performance.
(Training Commission, 1988, p. 15)

The concept of competence is thus inseparable from notions of anticipated
performance levels, and competence can clearly relate to just about any
conceivable aspect of human behaviour at work – behaviours, actions, personality
traits, understanding, skill, dealing with novelty, and the personal qualities brought
to interpersonal relationships. Conway and Powney (1990, p. 84) present a list of
competences expected in an adult educator, expressed mainly in terms of personal
attributes or characteristics, including self-awareness, open-mindedness, imagination, and belief in the potential of others. Despite the intuitive appeal of the idea,
the term competence does appear to lack precision in use.

A subsequent report prepared for the Training Agency by the consulting firm
Deloitte, Haskins and Sells (Smith *et al.*, 1989) highlighted a number of criticisms
of the narrow 'ability to perform' notion of competence. Other research (Institute
of Manpower Studies, 1984) has suggested that British managers tend to adopt a
narrow definition and skeptical view of management development as a whole,
compared with practice in America, Germany and Japan where investment in
management development is seen as a factor contributing to competitive success.
The preoccupation in Britain is more with the development of specific relevant
skills, rather than with effective work performance. Charles Handy (1987) reaches
much the same conclusions in his influential report, *The Making of Managers*.

Smith *et al.* (1989) cite two other criticisms of the competence concept, in effect
arguing that the concept has perhaps become too specific and precise in current
usage. Their remarks concern, respectively, the way in which the holistic expertise

of management is overlooked and the argument that competence is dependent on context. They cite a 1988 conference presentation from John Burgoyne who argued that:

> research and common sense show clearly that management is not the sequential exercise of discrete competences. Listings of separate competences at best simply illuminate different facets of what is at the end of the day a complex whole. (Smith *et al.*, 1989, p. 16)

Burgoyne has elsewhere voiced the argument that management activity involves the exercise of considerable measures of judgement, and that the task – and therefore the required competences – varies across different settings. The context-dependent nature of competence is reflected in the following quote from an Institute of Personnel Management spokesman (unidentified) challenging the simple listing of the attributes or qualities required of the competent manager:

> Significant research over many years has shown that there is no agreement on such general qualities and their relationship with managerial effectiveness. We believe that competence is dependent on the context in which it is demonstrated. (Smith *et al.*, 1989, p. 16)

Nevertheless, the Management Charter Initiative has proceeded to publish its competence-based standards for different levels of management. The middle-management standards published in 1990 identify four main management roles, ten units of competence, thirty-six elements of competence, and four personal competences (planning, managing others, managing oneself and using intellect). Each unit specifies the broad understanding required of the context, the appropriate management principles and techniques, and the specific information needs relevant to perform effectively in that unit of competence. The assessment scheme attached to this approach identifies 240 performance criteria for these elements, across 166 range indicators (range indicators are settings in which the competences can be expected to be demonstrated) (Management Charter Initiative, 1990, and Conway and Powney, 1990).

Andrew Thomson (1991), while broadly supporting the Management Charter Initiative (MCI), offers a balanced view of the development by identifying ten 'good things' and ten 'bad things' about it. The ten strengths are as follows:

1. Creation of a three-tier system of qualifications related to levels of management responsibility.
2. Generation of wider interest in management development.
3. Attention on management in general, not just high flyers.
4. Creation of generic standards of management competence.
5. Attempt to bridge the industry–education gap.
6. Creation of a nationally endorsed framework.
7. Provision for credit transfer.

8. Recognition and accreditation of prior learning.
9. Establishment of local employer networks.
10 Creation of greater professionalism in management.

Thomson then identifies ten criticisms.

1. The initiative is dominated by assessment at the expense of learning.
2. The knowledge and understanding base is not clearly specified.
3. The competence standards have been developed in a highly fragmented way with little attempt at systematic integration.
4. There is a lack of clarity concerning the relationship in practice between each level of standard and levels of management.
5. The standards specify a lowest common denominator, not the pursuit of excellence.
6. Assessment techniques are problematic.
7. Some of the distinctions between the levels of competence are marginal and difficult to specify in practice.
8. The institutions driving the initiative appear to have overlapping responsibilities.
9. The MCI itself has internal organizational problems.
10. The needs of a particular organization are not necessarily aligned with national standards.

Despite criticism of the management competence movement, we are about to report a study which sought to establish the competences of the effective change agent. The definition of competence adopted for the purposes of this study concerns actions and behaviours identified by change agents as contributing in their experience to the perceived effectiveness of change implementation. Content analysis of the diary transcripts revealed five competence clusters (or units) and fifteen specific attributes (elements) related to handling the project manager's process agenda. The five clusters were concerned with goal setting, role specification, communications, negotiating skills, and 'managing up' respectively. In summary these five clusters and fifteen attributes were as follows:

Goals
1. Sensitivity to changes in key personnel, top management perceptions, and market conditions, and to the way in which these impact the goals of the project in hand.
2. Clarity in specifying goals, in defining the achievable.
3. Flexibility in responding to changes outwith the control of the project manager, perhaps requiring major shifts in project goals and management style, and risk taking.

Roles
4. Team building abilities, to bring together key stakeholders and establish effective working groups, and clearly to define and delegate respective responsibilities.

5. Networking skills in establishing and maintaining appropriate contacts within and outside the organization.
6. Tolerance of ambiguity, to be able to function comfortably, patiently, and effectively in an uncertain environment.

Communication

7. Communication skills to transmit effectively to colleagues and subordinates the need for changes in project goals and in individual tasks and responsibilities.
8. Interpersonal skills, across the range, including selection, listening, collecting appropriate information, identifying the concerns of others, and managing meetings.
9. Personal enthusiasm, in expressing plans and ideas.
10. Stimulating motivation and commitment in others involved.

Negotiation

11. Selling plans and ideas to others, by creating a desirable and challenging vision of the future.
12. Negotiating with key players for resources, or for changes in procedures, and to resolve conflict.

Managing Up

13. Political awareness, in identifying potential coalitions, and in balancing conflicting goals and perceptions.
14. Influencing skills, to gain commitment to project plans and ideas from potential skeptics and resisters.
15. Helicopter perspective, to stand back from the immediate project and take a broader view of priorities.

In order to understand these fifteen attributes or competences more clearly, it is useful to consider typical and interesting examples from the diary analysis. The objective of the analysis was to identify behaviours, techniques or competences that contribute to effectiveness in the management of change in the perception of the change agent.

Goals 1   Sensitivity

Sensitivity to changes in key personnel, top management perceptions, and market conditions, and to the way in which these impact the goals of the project in hand

Action, and inaction, in an organization can have both predictable and unintended consequences. Project managers often find that issues could have been handled more effectively. However, hindsight is only available as an input to future decisions and change agents require sensitivity to issues and events that might influence progress. Examples of unintended consequences and the wisdom of hindsight are illustrated in the following diary entry from the Logic Manager, electronics manufacturing company:

> The decision to hold an initial strategy meeting was vital in establishing relationships, goals and plans. While kicking off the change in an ideal fashion, the lack of similar follow-on meetings contributed to misconceptions, political moves, and concerns over apparent shifts in power. If meetings had been held more regularly, some of the problems could have been highlighted and addressed in a more constructive manner.

In contrast, here from the diary of the Engineering Director, oil refining company, is an example of how lack of action by other key managers created problems for the project manager, and for the project:

> Another important area was that the marketing development for the project had not been carried out adequately if at all. In particular, even for the main products, the specifications had not been written down and a customer list prepared. When it came to by-products, the situation was one of almost complete vacuum in that marketing information with respect to what customers wanted, needed, could use, and what they were prepared to pay for them, was completely missing. The company was able to overcome part of these omissions by significant contributions from sales and technical people. A major loss to the company was that there were no attempts made to market the intermediate product which arose from the very first plant to be brought on line, until several months had elapsed. A keen and motivated marketing organization would have generated some cash flow by early sales from this source, while waiting for the higher-quality, higher-value products to emerge from the downstream plant.

Another example of change having unintended – and in this case desirable – consequences comes from this diary entry from the Director, land survey company:

> It might have been anticipated that the number of people involved in the company would have been reduced as a result of the introduction of new technology. However, the reverse has proven to be the case. The company has gradually grown from some two people in 1971 to some 100 people today [1989]. This has been a direct result of gradual diversification of its activities, mainly together with the incremental introduction of new technology throughout the business.

Goals 2   Clarity

Clarity in specifying goals, in defining the achievable

There are different ways of expressing goals, and there are different types of goal. We have touched previously on the need to be flexible in changing objectives and priorities in response to the changing context and to fresh problems and opportunities. But this does not overcome the consistent theme in the diary accounts concerning the need for a clear view of the nature and direction of change. Should that view have to change, then it has to be rearticulated and in similarly precise terms.

The importance of clarity of direction, and of vision, in defining the achievable is illustrated in this diary entry from the Chief Officer, probation service:

> The action group was helpful, went through my plan of action which is at a draft stage at the moment. My chief identified this issue, that it didn't really clarify, in the sense of going from A to B, what the B was, what the organization as a whole was, and I pointed out that what I'd done from my reading and comments on establishing vision and working to influence developments, it was important to be aware of the areas that you can influence and to concentrate on them. It didn't mean that the only person in the organization who could have any vision was the chief executive of the whole organization – you could have a vision of your area of work and seek to develop that. Really that's saying there needs to be a vision, a corporate strategy or whatever, for the organization as a whole, and then I can work within that, and I think he accepted that, recognized that was OK.

A similar sentiment is expressed in this entry from the diary of the Logic Manager, electronics manufacturing:

> People will accept change if they have a clear, well-communicated picture of the future where they can visualize a rewarding and satisfying role. However, if the direction cannot be forecast with any degree of certainty, people will follow and trust the participative and decisive leader rather than an autocrat.

Clarity and realism in project goal-setting is important for external relationships as well as for internal communications and motivation, as this diary entry from the Director, land survey company, illustrates with respect to attempts to seek external finance:

> The development of an appropriate, accurate as far as is practical, business plan is what these organizations seem to obtain, and the only way of raising

such money is to develop an appropriate business plan. There is little point in going along to discuss the outlines of things. Rather than wasting the other person's time and your own, it is important to have an appropriate business plan prior to instigating discussions with prospective targets for additional finance.

Clarity is inadequate on its own. Objectives have to be realistic, and have to be seen to be realistic, and projects founder where goals are too ambitious or are simply not achievable:

A major drawback was that, for a small family company with no experience of implementing a complex project, there was an inadequate allowance of time for teething problems to be overcome. Of course, time equates to expense. The small company management do not appreciate that large, modern process plants are complex in design and layout and need many many weeks of familiarization, by skilled operators, before they can be operated efficiently. For this project, there seemed to be the idea that, once the plant was mechanically complete, then it was simply a case of pushing a button and product would flow. Of course, in the real world nothing could be further from the truth.

This diary entry is from the Engineering Director, oil company. The ability to define the achievable, in the organizational context, and to articulate this clearly, is thus a critical component of effective project management.

Goals 3   Flexibility

Flexibility in responding to changes outwith the control of the project manager, perhaps requiring major shifts in project goals and management style, and risk taking
Large and complex projects inevitably never run as they were planned, and the change agent can expect a series of more or less intractable issues and problems to resolve, such as these, from the diary of the Engineering Director, oil refining:

As well as progressing the construction of the refinery, the small team at the main site was developing the process technology for the refining of the extract products. An adequate process for the by-products arising from the pre-treatment plant did not avail itself to the project team in time for the refinery completion, and this had to be 'cobbled together' from some redundant equipment after the refinery was up and running. This was an unsatisfactory situation but nonetheless one which had to be accepted by everyone concerned since there had been insufficient time to develop all the necessary technology in fine detail. We then had to resort to taking some significant risks in some important areas.

One disappointment and, I believe, a significant factor in the project, was that just before commissioning the manager of the pilot plant development team was transferred to another job. He had been promised to me at the project inception and I had 'designed' him into the working operation.

Another example of the need for a flexible response to unforeseen events and problems is illustrated in this diary entry from the Logic Manager, electronics company:

Assumptions at the beginning of the change over-simplified the difficulty in entering this type of market. Essentially the new business demanded a different mindset for senior managment and also a different company culture. Previously the company had been involved in high-volume, low-cost production, emphasizing yields and costs. Would they have entered the business had they appreciated the true difficulties and time-scale required to establish this new function? In a change such as this, details cannot be determined at the start of the project. Should management therefore take a more realistic view about the future and set less formidable goals?

Flexibility also involves an element of risk, and there may in many cases be a need clearly to identify and accept the risks associated with different possible lines of action, as illustrated in this diary entry from the Systems Manager, public utility:

So I arrived at seven alternatives, each with different costs, each with similar benefits but with different discounted cash flow over a five-year period. Clearly there is a certain amount of uncertainty about information, uncertainty of the accuracy of information. We don't have complete knowledge so clearly there is a risk involved. The question comes to how to measure that risk and the different degrees of risk between each of the options.

The following diary entry, from the Logic Manager, electronics manufacturing, indicates how dealing with risk uncertainty of this kind may be a matter of leadership or management style:

Change has altered the structure, roles and staff levels for the UK group. Middle management had to deploy the various skills in altering these to suit the situation, both current and future. From this observation, it can be concluded that a manager involved in change needs to deal with numerous issues simultaneously and a variety of skills are necessary. The ability to adapt style and technique as demanded by the situation was also necessary. Flexibility, patience and tolerance are required.

Roles 1   Team building

Team building abilities, to bring together key stakeholders and establish effective working groups, and clearly to define and delegate respective responsibilities

Larger-scale projects are rarely the sole responsibility of one individual, and typically involve a number of stakeholders, or players, who may constitute a more or less formal steering group or project team. Not surprising then to find a number of diary entries commenting on the need for team-building abilities, such as this from the diary of the Engineering Director, oil refinery:

> An important feature of the project was to weld the staff together as a team and to ensure that they all had adequate training in order to run the refinery efficiently and safely.
>
> Some of the staff taken on were mature with good solid experience gained in the oil industry, chemical industry, on the Ayrshire coast or the Forth estuary. As well as the seasoned operatives, we decided that we would take on younger, graduate-type employees who had little experience but lots of energy and enthusiasm.

Decisions concerning team composition and leadership are also critical. Consciously arranged 'critical events' in the early life of the team can be a useful way to cement working relationships and help build team cohesiveness, as this entry from the diary of the Logic Manager, electronics manufacturing, suggests:

> The applications specific integrated circuits (ASIC) division was set up to handle all full and semi-custom activities. The semi-custom market place was identified as a growing opportunity and the technology demanded leading-edge software which enabled customers to design circuits effectively without a need to understand device physics. For these reasons, and due to the company's limited experience in this market, it was decided to hire a new Vice President to head this division. The person chosen was a highly regarded professional from the computer industry who had been in charge of overseeing his own company's ASIC strategy. It was perceived that hiring a manager from the user community would help the division to develop quickly products that users required. Very soon after the division was established, the manager called for a one-week brainstorming–team-building session in Geneva. All the managers of the various groups directly reporting to the Vice President participated, including representatives from the European business group and the manager of the development group in Scotland. As a result of this meeting, relationships were established and objectives were agreed. The Geneva meeting was seen as a major benefit by the participants and the

manager felt excited about the possibility of getting his team involved in state of the art developments.

The third phase concentrated on building smaller groups which were functionally complete with the exception of marketing, although individuals have been assigned to work with specific groups. This integration, in conjunction with a leader who believes in delegating power downwards in the organization, has helped to create a more effective and more enjoyable environment to work in. This has helped to develop a sense of pride in the work delegated to individuals and has been confirmed by the enthusiasm displayed in my own group.

Asked for advice based on his change management experience, the Management Services Manager, local authority, put this entry in his diary:

Where possible, select a good development team to work with. Ensure that they are fully aware of the remit of the project and that they work to it, encourage in as many ways as possible, take them into your confidence and instil in them the importance of their contribution to the project.

Roles 2   Networking

Networking skills in establishing and maintaining appropriate contacts within and outside the organization

Large-scale projects often involve a number of different stakeholders within the organization, in other sections and perhaps at other locations, amd may also involve people and organizations outside, such as consultants, contractors, and suppliers. It can be useful, if time consuming, for the change agent consciously to maintain these personal contacts, even though they may not be formally necessary at any one point in time:

On the original point about contacting colleagues in other probation areas to see how they worked, I'll have a chat with a few people who may be able to identify the best people to talk to and perhaps arrange a couple of visits to go and talk it through with them. I think it will be useful visiting Devon, and perhaps Nottingham and Leicestershire. I think I'll have a chat with a few people about some other potential contacts, and I'll give it a try, actually detailing what it is I want to do on those interviews to try and actually build that into the report that I'll do for the County Council Managing the '90s project.

This is a diary entry from the Chief Officer, probation service, echoing the advice of Rosabeth Moss Kanter from Chapter 3 concerning coalition building and 'power skills' in maintaining support and anticipating resistance.

Roles 3   Tolerance of ambiguity

Tolerance of ambiguity, to be able to function comfortably, patiently, and effectively in an uncertain environment

This diary entry from the Director, land survey company, illustrates the typical uncertainty generated in projects in quadrant four:

> While the [new computing system] introduced into the company was successful, the period of time taken to bring the facility into production exceeded initial expectations by a substantial margin. The initial claims made by [the supplier] for the product itself were optimistic rather than misleading. It took some twelve to eighteen months to finally overcome the majority of the software 'bugs' which had to be resolved in order that the product be of use to the company.

Such events are often outwith the control or influence of the project manager who nevertheless has to be able to live with the consequent delays and disappointments.

The project manager may often also have to accept the risks involved in significant technical and organizational change, as this entry also from the diary of the Director, land survey company, shows:

> [The company] identified this as an opportunity to apply its skills in survey and computerized mapping applications. It became involved in developing a system to convert maps into digital form in 1983 and has been involved in the Ordnance Survey's conversion programme since that date. Plainly there has been a requirement to make a major investment in putting a system together, acquiring and training people to develop the necessary human and physical resources in order to provide the necessary service to the Ordnance Survey. The investment has been large for a company in its infancy, and the risks very high.

Communication 1   Communication skills

Communication skills to transmit effectively to colleagues and subordinates the need for changes in project goals and in individual tasks and responsibilities

Given the range of diary entries commenting on the need to balance task and technology orientation with people skills, it is again not surprising to find a number of entries concerning the need for effective communications. The fact that these issues are now widely accepted and understood does not undermine their enduring importance. One typical entry from the diary of the Logic Manager, electronics manufacturing, was:

> Good communication and the involvement of representatives from all affected groups are mandatory for commitment. Also, politics is more likely to be a factor if communication is not handled efficently. If strategy is left to filter through, problems will result. Individuals with perceived positions of power can impose their own strategies to achieve their own political desires. Communication is vital. More information should be made available to more people at all levels. Especially important is the ability to be able to listen to ideas from lower levels in the organization.

This diary entry illustrates some of the problems of inadequate communication about project progress, from the Engineering Director, oil refinery:

> The management responsibility for the project tended to be through myself reporting directly to the Managing Director. In this respect, it was apparent to me that he did not communicate the main issues which arose during the course of the project to his Board. For example, when we reviewed the capital requirements with our contractor, it was some weeks later that I discovered that the rest of the Board had not been told of our decision to reduce the capacity in order to reduce capital cost. While the whole Board ostensibly retained responsibility for the project, in fact they tended to be uninvolved to the extent that they relied on the Managing Director's judgement.

The concept 'communication' is thus here an umbrella term for a wide range of management activities and behaviour. Some of the other attributes or competences identified in this analysis, such as negotiating skills or networking, can also be regarded simply as specific aspects of communication skills. However, the analysis highlighted both those specific dimensions and the generalized importance of communications, and it was felt appropriate to incorporate this.

Communication 2   Interpersonal skills

Interpersonal skills, across the range, including selection, listening, collecting appropriate information, identifying the concerns of others, and managing meetings

The comments just made with respect to the place of communications in this analysis apply equally to interpersonal skills. Once again, it would be reasonable to point out that many of the issues identified here are dimensions of interpersonal skill – such as influencing, selling, and personal enthusiasm. The diary analysis, however, identified both specific components and the general importance of these issues. Some aspects of interpersonal process are straightforward, as the project manager becomes involved in the details of, for example, recruitment as this entry from the diary of the Engineering Director, oil refining company, shows:

> In early 1985, I personally started to recruit the staff required for the refinery, beginning with the current refinery manager who was to be my main assistant for the commissioning period. We also recruited the shift supervisors and operatives and the other specialists who would be required.

However, the breadth of competence in this area, as with communications, is wide and is reflected in the diary entry of the Director, land survey company:

> The third lesson, and possibly equally as important as the other two, is not to have managers, directors or others so involved in the technology and hardware/software itself that they can't manage people. They just don't have the time. Rather than training a manager to become experienced and understand the hardware that he is going to run, it is far more important that he has an overview of the equipment hardware/software and he realises what the targets are and what it is he is trying to achieve with the new equipment.

This generally accepted position is supported by this entry in the diary of the Logic Manager, electronics manufacturing:

> Successful promoters [of change] have been shown in this study to have skills in the following. Planning and tracking; analysing situations; influencing; negotiating; conflict resolution; dealing with potential political motivations. Each of the three major promoters involved had different management styles and they all tended to hire or promote those with similar outlooks. The behavioural characteristics have definitely shown that in the long term the promoters need to be concerned as much with the people as the task.

Communication 3   Personal enthusiasm

Personal enthusiasm, in expressing plans and ideas

Change agents faced with apparently insurmountable difficulties are advantaged by the ability to make progress regardless, through their own energy, persistence, and enthusiasm. This is illustrated in a diary entry from the Engineering Director, oil refinery:

> We encountered very significant difficulties in the first three months of 1986, and experienced many problems with fouling and blocking of process lines, with loss of solvent and wastage of oils, etc. These were difficult days for

everybody concerned, particularly myself, since it involved working almost continuously at the refinery every day for a period from September 1985 until about April 1986. These days were long and demanding and for someone my age physically demanding. Even the younger men found it difficult to maintain attention and enthusiasm.

This entry from the diary of the Director, land survey company, reinforces this point:

The organization as a whole had selected a piece of software and hardware that they thought was going to work, and once they had it installed, they found all sorts of difficulties. They could at that stage have decided, OK, this was just too much to handle and they couldn't get over it. However, I think because of the personalities, because of their determination to succeed and diversify, the installation became a two-way thing. The [suppliers] were aware that we were prepared to push this thing through and were really anxious to ensure that it succeeded, and they became involved in a development and a big hand-holding operation, so it became a two-way deal so that together we made this product which had, apparently, been introduced into the marketplace too early, succeed.

Enthusiasm can be infectious, and the change agent can exploit this.

Communication 4   Stimulating motivation and commitment

Stimulating motivation and commitment in others involved

Large-scale change in organizations typically evolves over lengthy periods of time, and can be frustrating when anticipated events and results fail to materialize on schedule. The enthusiasm generated at the beginning of a project of change can thus evaporate through time, particulary where progress is slower than was planned and anticipated. The change agent has to be as aware of the need to manage enthusiasm as of the need to anticipate and block resistance. This can mean acting to restore motivation and commitment when necessary, as this diary entry from the Logic Manager, electronics manufacturing, suggests:

As the system progressed, the middle management role of the design manager became more difficult. The engineers themselves were concerned with the future, were frustrated with system inadequacies and the cell development task did not utilize their skills or knowledge. The manager's role, therefore, was concerned with day-to-day motivation. It was at this stage that the manager began to review the situation with a view to moving some engineers into other groups and altering the staff to obtain people suitable to the expected future roles.

This aspect of the change agent's role can also be related to team building, as this diary entry from the Business Manager, computer manufacturing, illustrates:

> We managed to gather our European staff team together in Ireland on October 6 for about six hours and we did a presentation on order fulfilment, as I have already described. It was clear, after about the first hour, that we had managed to capture the interest, imagination and energy of the group, and very clearly they were going to try and find a way, even although we have no formal budget to make a scheduling programme happen. It was an excellent culmination of fifteen months' work, though in many ways it was just the beginning.

Effectiveness in this respect can therefore be challenging and satisfying, and can stimulate individuals to find ways around organizational barriers as this latter entry suggests.

Negotiation 1   Selling plans and ideas

Selling plans and ideas to others, by creating a desirable and challenging vision of the future

The change agent is frequently involved in attempts to 'sell' ideas and plans to other organizational members, using strategies that include open communication and participation as well as conscious manipulation of information and the message that is being conveyed. Some of this selling is conducted in more or less informal settings, as this diary entry from the Chief Officer, probation service, suggests:

> Next week is about leadership and working with change. An opportunity for me there to take some risks perhaps and work with individuals, carrying forward ideas which they may find difficulty with. So I will make a point to work on that, to use the week particularly for that.

Some of this selling, however, may involve somewhat more devious approaches to standard organizational operating procedures, to enable the project manager to achieve quickly and painlessly the desired results. One illustration of this comes from the Technical Director, engineering company:

> Having made the decision to buy the equipment it was then only necessary to justify its purchase. Use of a computer programme to calculate internal rate of return on discounted cash flow helped me considerably, enabling 'what if?' calculations to be made. It was therefore possible to project that the

increasing workload of the company anticipated in three years would require the employment of a new draughtsman. This employment could be avoided by the installation of the computer aided draughting equipment. It was considered that this was a low-risk justification, and would be difficult to prove correct or otherwise.

This is consistent with comments in Chapter 3 concerning the need for balance between public performance and backstage activity, and for contextually acceptable behaviour on the part of the change agent, particularly with respect to legitimating the changes proposed.

Negotiation 2   Negotiating with key players

Negotiating with key players for resources, or for changes in procedures, and to resolve conflict

The project manager typically has to drive at least some aspect of change – if not the project as a whole – against competition from other sections of the organization and other individuals pursuing their own projects and priorities. The resources required are thus not always going to be readily provided, demanding negotiating ability on the part of the project manager. This is reinforced by a diary entry from the Logic Manager, electronics manufacturing:

> A lot of the manager's time was spent negotiating with senior management in the States to win charters for such projects. The manager's role was therefore changed to promote another change and involved negotiating with top management to gain agreement and then selling the concept to the engineers and having them regard it as both a challenge and a required need.

The problems of success confronting the change agent, thus opening up other areas for negotiation, are illustrated in this diary entry from the Engineering Director, oil refinery:

> It was evident that, as the Kilpatrick refinery consumed more and more capital and recruited the 'high quality' operatives needed to run the more sophisticated hardware, then polarization developed between the two sites. This polarization occurred through the offices of the Operations Director of the day. He could see the Kilpatrick operation becoming effective and then started to take an increasing interest in personnel matters and to exert influence over the way the refinery was operated (although, in fact, he was technically not competent to do so). Nonetheless, this had a detrimental effect on relationships and caused frustrations and irritations among my staff at

Kilpatrick because it was fairly obvious that even the Managing Director tended to defer to his Operations Director in major decisions about personnel. The MD did not wish to upset his senior directors, hence the Kilpatrick refinery tended to be stuck with some of the outmoded systems and practices that [the older refinery] had had to suffer over the years.

Managing up 1 Political awareness

Political awareness, in identifying potential coalitions, and in balancing conflicting goals and perceptions

The goals of the change agent may not always be seen as consistent with the goals of other stakeholders or players in the organization and may in some circumstances be regarded as suspect. It may be appropriate for the politically aware change agent to take action to change such perceptions where they may adversely affect the project, as this diary entry from the Chief Officer, probation service implies:

> Another issue we considered was the fact that what I am proposing within the project obviously has career opportunities for me and therefore is likely to be seen as threatening by people within my office. I discussed that with the action group. That was helpful because I have been concerned in the past that what I was doing in terms of acting as a change agent comes across as empire building.

Another key aspect of 'managing up' concerns relationships with senior company officers who may see change agents as useful sources of expertise, and as sources of legitimation for specific decisions. This is illustrated in the following diary extract from the Engineering Director, oil refinery:

> My other role is a sort of right-hand man to the Managing Director. To give him the necessary support and confidence (which he already had in large measure). I sought to ensure that we could go forward to obtain the necessary finance. His past experience of raising money hadn't been very good as a result of the relative immaturity of the market, a young and growing organization, taken together with the perceived level of risk attached to the works. My involvement was really in the role of right-hand man, to answer queries, to provide support, to go along to meetings and to assist the MD through these meetings and generally to help where there was any confusion and to smooth the way . . . to let the MD feel that at least the decisions he had made had been clearly thought through. I became a sort of sounding board to shoot off ideas or to widen his view.

Managing up 2   Influencing skills

Influencing skills, to gain commitment to project plans and ideas from potential skeptics and resisters

This can clearly be seen as another dimension of either communication or of interpersonal skills. The diary content analysis, however, suggested that it was sufficiently significant to be identified separately, and the audio diarists in debriefing supported this view. One illustration of this attribute comes from the following diary entry from the Engineering Director, oil refinery:

> In an ideal world, the Board members would have been more experienced in the process industries to the extent that they could better gauge the crisis and the enormous step which the company had to take in order to achieve success. This is a peculiar part of this project in that, in my own role, having had nearly thirty years experience with sophisticated companies in the process industries such as ICI and Du Pont, I was in a much better position to appreciate the potential hazards and pitfalls of biting off this huge project than any of the Board.

The change agent, as in this case, is often forced to seek to exercise influence by virtue of superior expertise, and not through managerial authority. This position is reflected in the organizational behaviour literature as the distinction between expert power on the one hand and position power on the other (see Huczynski and Buchanan, 1991, pp. 494–6 for a discussion of managerial power bases). Change agents in organic organizations in particular have to seek cooperation from those over whom they have no direct managerial authority, have to negotiate resources in competition with colleagues and superiors, and have to seek the collaboration, support and commitment from those in sections and positions outwith their own spheres of responsibility. Influencing skills are critical in such settings.

Managing up 3   Helicopter perspective

Helicopter perspective, to stand back from the immediate project and take a broader view of priorities

This final dimension of 'managing up' seems particularly important in the context of strategic technological and organizational changes, where the perspective and vision of the change agent presumably has to be wider, broader, and longer term. The change agent may need to strike a balance between the day to day routine of problem solving and the long term 'helicopter' view of developments. Useful here to remember that from a helicopter one obtains, first, a good overview of the ground directly beneath and, second, a good forward view of the horizon.

The significance of the helicopter perspective is indicated in this diary entry from the Director, land survey company:

> Training should therefore be targeted at the lowest level to ensure that those people who are going to be running the equipment on a day-to-day basis will develop an expertise beyond that of the manager in the running of the equipment, and should be as rigorous as possible, and that the manager changes his role and learns to take a much wider view of the business than traditionally he would have done.

Shifting sands, interconnectedness, top management view and problems with perceived ownership of change processes make a number of demands on the project manager. From the analysis of the audio diary accounts, it is suggested that these demands group under the five principal headings of goals, roles, communication, negotiation and managing up. The fifth category, managing up, incorporates aspects of the other four clusters, but represents the exercise of those competences in a different and significant context, and thus merits allocation to a distinct category.

The demands identified here are not new, and are in many respects traditional. There appear, however, to be two emerging aspects in this otherwise traditional list of competences, concerning emphasis and packaging. First, our audio diarists, when presented with the 'so what's new about this?' argument said that in their experience change management now placed a stronger emphasis on these five competence clusters, and that traditional project management and content agenda skills were relatively less important. Second, they argued that effective change implementation requires this 'package' of process agenda competences, reinforcing our earlier comments about establishing priorities across the control, content and process agendas, and in the process agenda establishing a balance between public performance and backstage activity in managing and constructing an appropriate and contextually acceptable change implementation process.

The image of the change agent which emerges from this analysis is of an individual exercising considerable interpersonal, social, organizational and political skills. This is the result that could be expected given the discussion in Chapter 2 about managing in a high vulnerability context, and from the discussion in Chapter 3 about the social and political dynamics of change processes in organizations. This is not the image of the project manager with deep technical or content understanding and project planning, budgeting and costing capabilities. The ability to manage organizational networks appears to be more valuable then the ability to understand, say, electronic networks. The ability to influence perceptions and negotiate appropriate resources appears to be more valuable than the ability to control costs and establish appropriate deadlines.

Nevertheless, what we have done here is simply to produce another list of management competences, similar in style to the 'units and elements' approach criticized earlier. Clearly this listing and classifying of management competences is a game that anyone can play, with broadly similar results. We have been playing this game ourselves; a somewhat different interpretation of the same data is used in the companion volume to this text (Boddy and Buchanan, 1992). Where is the added value in the classification presented here? First, this analysis has concentrated on the competences of change agents, and not on management in general. Second, the analysis relies on first-hand accounts of change projects given by the managers responsible for them. Third, we have confirmation here that the competences of the change agent can be identified and expressed in a relatively straightforward manner. Fourth, we offer this analysis, not as the definitive account of a simple formula for change management success, but as one element in a rather more elaborate, but still practically useful, model. We will explore further limitations of this approach once we have examined the extent to which survey data confirm these competences as useful.

Survey confirmation

In the survey, the conduct of which was explained in Chapter 2, respondents were asked to rate the contribution to project success of thirty different skills and competences. In terms of the five competence clusters – goals, communication, negotiation and managing up – responses are shown in Tables 4.1–4.5.

Table 4.1 Goals: rating of various skills and competences (% response)

Skills and competences	Very helpful	Somewhat helpful	Not at all helpful
Ability to get agreement on clear and acceptable goals	83	12	4
Concentration on implementation of the plan, without being side-tracked by dissenting views	54	33	13
Recognition of the implications of changes elsewhere	54	40	6
Revision of strategies as conditions changed	46	38	16
Ensuring objectives take account of other interests	40	47	13

The results in Table 4.1 provide support for the importance of the sensitivity, clarity and flexibility identified from the diary analysis in relation to project goals. Agreement with the last four items in the table is mixed, again indicating wider variation in experience in the survey sample than with the eight diarists.

Table 4.2 Roles: rating of various skills and competences (% response)

Skills and competences	Very helpful	Somewhat helpful	Not at all helpful
Early clarification of who was responsible for each part of the job	73	22	4
Ensuring other staff understood their own roles adequately	63	32	4
Ensuring the various groups working on the change worked well together	61	33	5
Ability to deal with personality clashes within the team	60	35	5
Encouraging a project team to work in harmony with related groups	59	37	4
Key players altering/expanding their role as necessary, to cover key aspects of the task	54	37	10
Establishing links with other groups to define the scope of the change	35	50	15

Also in Table 4.2 the results offer mixed support for the importance of team building and networking capabilities, and little support for tolerance of ambiguity as a key attribute. Clarification of responsibility at an early stage was a highly rated factor. The percentage of responses in the 'not helpful' category, however, reach 15 per cent in only one item, concerning networking issues.

Again, in Table 4.3, the percentage of responses in the 'not helpful' category is low, not exceeding 8 per cent on any item. While communications in general are rated as important, role clarity shows as significant again, particularly with respect to the first of these items, concerning communication across other departments to be affected by project implementation.

The low level of strong agreement in Table 4.4 with the item concerning 'working within resources' highlights the importance of negotiating skills, also indicated in the level of agreement with the first item in the table. Selling skills also receive support with low percentage responses in the 'not helpful' category.

Response to the first item in Table 4.5 highlights the perceived importance of the 'helicopter perspective', and the need for political awareness also appears to be widely recognized. Two issues that emerge as critically important from the last three items in the table concern senior management sanction or 'sponsorship', and keeping senior management up to date on progress. As with the other four clusters, strong, but mixed, support is provided for the need for skill and competence in 'managing up'.

There are a number of problems with this competence-based analysis of the role of the change agent. There are four such problems in particular.

Table 4.3 Communication: rating of various skills and competences (% response)

Skills and competences	Very helpful	Somewhat helpful	Not at all helpful
Ensuring that each department involved knew what was expected of them	81	17	2
Ensuring staff understood the reasons for the change	75	21	4
Improving communication between different people involved in the change	71	27	2
Making sure that staff were aware of how the parts of the change linked together	63	32	4
Ensuring that strategy was conveyed to all concerned	62	33	5
Keeping those affected up to date with changing project goals	60	36	4
Actively seeking information about changes affecting the project	55	36	8

Table 4.4 Negotiation: rating of various skills not competences (% response)

Skills and competences	Very helpful	Somewhat helpful	Not at all helpful
Securing adequate resources for the change	77	21	2
Ensuring people affected saw benefits of value to them	69	27	4
Reaching mutual agreement with interested parties about targets and objectives	62	33	5
Negotiating new arrangements to cope with temporary difficulties	35	55	10
Working within the resources originally made available to the project	25	50	25

First, the survey findings offer equivocal support for the generalizability of the audio diary analysis. The diary data rely on a very small sample of change agents who, by virtue of their participation in this study, were working on quadrant four change projects in their respective organizations. The survey drew on a considerably wider cross section of experience and, as indicated in Chapter 2,

Table 4.5 Managing up: rating of various skills and competences (% response)

Skills and competences	Very helpful	Somewhat helpful	Not at all helpful
Ability to visualize how all the dimensions of the project fitted together	74	24	2
Awareness that agreement would be needed between different interests	60	34	6
Anticipation of how one decision or change could affect people's attitudes to the whole change.	51	42	7
Taking responsibility for dealing with all aspects of the project, without requiring senior management support	33	35	30
Managing the project despite the lack of a sponsor among top management	30	18	52
Not troubling senior management with details of the project's progress	17	34	49

different experience from different contexts highlights different issues and generates this wider variety of responses to the survey questionnaire.

Second, the fifteen competences identified are not comparable. They constitute an incongruous mix of skills, cognitive styles and personality traits. While some of these can be developed with training and practice, such as communications and negotiating skills, it is not clear how to develop attributes such as personal enthusiasm and tolerance of ambiguity. It is also not clear from such a listing of competences how they are interrelated, either in theory or in practice, although there is clearly overlap between the distinct categories identified here.

Third, it is the ability to use those competences appropriately that counts, not so much the mere possession of this odd collection of attributes. This analysis gives no indication of how these competences apply to managing the process of change in different contexts. It was argued in Chapter 3 that competences cannot be understood independently of the process in which the change agent engages. That process varies from context to context, and so the demands made on the change agent vary. This, or any other similar, list of fifteen competences is idealized, presented as it is here in such a context-free manner.

Fourth, this list of competences can be seen as a set of general management attributes, not peculiar to project management, and not new. When presented with this argument in debriefing, our diarists indicated agreement. However, they also argued that the context in which they were managing placed a higher premium on these attributes, as indicated earlier, and that possession of this 'package' of attributes had become, for them, critical. This does not detract entirely from the view that, in the perspective developed here, the competences of the change agent would appear to be straightforward and unremarkable.

That list of competences, therefore, is nothing more than a tool-kit. It says nothing about how these competences are to be most effectively applied. It says nothing of how they might relate to the issues of public performance and backstage activity discussed earlier. It says nothing about how they relate either to the process of change or to the context of change. As argued in Chapter 3, it is difficult to understand and express the competence of the change agent independently of the change process. Expertise, on the other hand, can be seen to involve the appropriate application of this 'tool-kit' to the management of that process in a given context.

Tools for analysis and guides to action

How do you meet the challenge of change?

1. Through 'informed opportunism' – set the direction, not the detailed strategy.
2. Information creates competitive advantage; flexibility is the chief strategic weapon.
3. Individuals are the main source of renewal; 'directed autonomy' with 'friendly facts and congenial controls'. Set the boundaries, and get out of the way.
4. How do others really see you? Check with customers, competitors, suppliers, employees. Look constantly into 'the different mirrors'.
5. Foster teamwork and trust.
6. Bust the bureaucracy; security of employment, but not of position. Build momentum into the culture.
7. Expect a lot and get a lot; the 'Pygmalion Effect'.
8. Get commitment to exciting causes. (Based on R. H. Waterman, 1987)

The management of change is an area that has lent itself to easy prescription. We made this observation in Chapter 1. However, we also saw how processual and contextual analyses revealed the multi-layered and multivariate nature of change, indicating the central role of legitimacy, the importance of ritual and symbolic action, and the significance of cultural and historical factors. We also noted in Chapter 1 that one of the problems in this field could lie in lack of easily assimilated practical advice – not lack of advice to the change agent per se. We have been critical of project management materials for their advocacy of an unrealistic linear model of the change process. We were critical of participative management materials for their naivety in assuming that involvement necessarily leads to agreement and commitment. We have been critical of sociological accounts for their complexity and lack of clear prescription. It would seem that the models on offer from, for example, Johnson, Doz and Prahalad, and Pettigrew, offer valuable tools for analysis, of value to the researcher planning longer-term longitudinal study of change processes at different levels in the organization. On the other hand, the advice from Goodwin Watson on overcoming resistance, or from Dexter Dunphy on characteristics of effective change, or from Rosabeth Moss Kanter on how to define your project, or from Peter Keen on counter-counter-implementation, offer simple practical advice for the change agent, leaving aside the complications of context, culture and history.

Tools for analysis are thus not necessarily good practical guides to action; tools for action do not always stimulate interesting research agendas, and may not reflect adequately the underlying theory or understanding. The problem, clearly, is to find the middle ground, by basing practical guidance on a sound understanding of the processes and context, by relating theoretical models to realistic prescriptions for action.

So, how do we understand the expertise of the contemporary change agent, particularly the manager operating with an organic management system and with a change programme in quadrant four?

First, we have sought to establish that this expertise covers three agendas, concerning the content of change, the control of change, and the process of change. Each of these agendas is concerned with a different unfolding logic, of problem solving, of ownership, and of legitimacy respectively. Second, we have also sought to establish that the agenda priorities of the change agent are contingent on context. We have claimed that the content and control agendas assume high and medium priority respectively in low vulnerability contexts, and that process and control agendas assume such priorities in high vulnerability contexts. Third, we have argued that the change agent must activate and balance appropriate public and backstage activities to legitimate change, maintain personal credibility, and sustain adequate support for proposals, while acting within the local norms and culture of the organization.

The process of change, in context, is thus socially constructed through the actions of the change agent. Many accounts of change have the project manager or change agent 'working through' the change process or the implementation life cycle. In the perspective offered here, the change agent is actively responsible for shaping, managing or for socially constructing the change process through which the organization is moved. This construction involves the change agent in determining the public performance – what, how, who and when. This simultaneously involves managing the support for that public performance through backstage activities of the kind explored in Chapter 3. A series of judgements is required of the change agent concerning, for example, the acceptability of propositions about or arguments for change. It is rarely seen to be legitimate to support change on the basis of personal gain. It is on the other hand legitimate for others to ask, 'what's in it for the change agent?' The change agent is thus also involved in the social construction of the process of change in judgements about timing, about the presentation of plans and ideas, and about who will accept what, at what stage, with what reasoning, and with what reaction.

This construction is at the same time shaped by the context, and by the realities of current cultural constraints, current political issues, and past history and experience. The change agent constructs this process, through time, faced with these facilitating and constraining contextual issues, through the mechanisms of communication, justification, presentation, legitimation and negotiation – some front of house, some backstage. These are all well-understood, and eminently trainable, management skills. However, given that the effectiveness of the change agent is dependent on the organization's past history and current political and cultural realities, the 'expertise' of the change agent is also contextual – dependent on the specific setting. The action of the change agent in context must be both effective and acceptable. Effectiveness and acceptability are context dependent, so our understanding of change agency 'expertise' must also be context dependent.

We would thus like to propose a two-layer model of expertise for the change agent as follows:

Level 1   Concerns diagnostic skills, judgemental capability, and behavioural flexibility. These concern developing an understanding of the changing context, identifying agenda priorities, and acting accordingly – public and backstage – to construct an effective and acceptable change process.

Level 2   Includes the fifteen competences in five clusters identified and illustrated in this chapter. These concern relatively well defined and well understood management behaviours for which effective management development approaches have been long estabished.

Level 2 concerns the 'tool-kit', or what might be described as core competences. Level 1 concerns managerial judgement. We have sought to establish that the core competences are necessary, and although they are unremarkable, they are not sufficient, in the creation of change agency expertise. The effective change agent is able to deploy those core competences appropriately in context, and is not merely able to display those individual competences separately. Expertise in this field thus involves the ability to combine those core competences effectively and appropriately with managerial judgement. We will explore in the next and final chapter how this two-dimensional expertise can be developed.

What practical advice can we begin to extract from the argument of this book? How can we begin to move towards tools for action – or even broad guidelines for action? This would seem to revolve around an understanding of the relationship between context and agenda priorities.

First, in a low vulnerability context, content and control agendas take priority, the critical competences of the project manager lie with technical expertise and the use of conventional control techniques, and the process agenda and related competences are less significant. The dominant unfolding logic is that of problem solving. Project management models of the change process, and advice set in that frame, are likely to be perceived as relevant and realistic. The competences identified in this chapter are useful in this context, but not critical to the perceived effectiveness of the change agent.

Second, in a high vulnerability context, process and control agendas take priority, the critical competences of the project manager involve a combination of change management expertise and the use of control techniques, and the content agenda becomes less significant. The dominant unfolding logics are those of legitimacy and ownership. Processual models of change, and advice set in that frame, are more likely to be perceived relevant and realistic. The project manager with no prior skill or expertise in the content of the change can be effective in this context, especially where that expertise is available in the project team. Appropriate deployment of the competences identified in this chapter, directed towards political intervention of the kind identified in Chapter 3, is thus more critical to the perceived effectiveness of the change agent.

Third, from the perspective of the employing organization, it would appear prudent to select project managers with strengths in the content and control areas for low vulnerability contexts. Appraisal and reward in a low vulnerability context are likely to be based on technical achievements, and on ability to manage the implementation in accordance with time and resource budgets. For projects in a high vulnerability context, on the other hand, it would seem more appropriate to select project managers who can combine knowledge of project planning and control techniques with process skills concerning goals, roles, communication, negotiation and managing up. Project managers in a high vulnerability context are more appropriately appraised and rewarded on their ability to implement change with support and commitment – 'bringing the organization with them' – rather than on technical competence.

Fourth, the implications for the individual can be expressed in similar terms. The project manager with technical expertise and competence in control techniques, but lacking process skills, would be better advised to avoid high vulnerability contexts or to seek appropriate training (given that some of the process competences identified are personality traits, not trainable skills). In contrast, the project manager weak in technical expertise, but competent with the control agenda and strong in process skills should avoid low vulnerability contexts where content deficiencies are likely to be exposed.

Fifth, management development programmes for project managers should take into account context expectations, with process skills given more prominence for those expected to encounter high vulnerability contexts. Many project management development courses concentrate on 'the staple fare', on control agenda techniques which, while useful, do not adequately equip project managers with the broader-based competences they may need. This argument has so far assumed that it is possible for the project manager to avoid working in high vulnerability contexts. That assumption may be false. It is with management development issues that the next and final chapter is concerned.

5

Management development strategies

The expertise of the change agent

Management training is defined as the process by which managers acquire the knowledge and skills related to their work requirements by formal, structured or guided means. Management education is the structured, formal learning process which often takes place in an institutional framework. Management development is the broader concept concerned with developing the individual rather than emphasizing the learning of narrowly defined skills; it is a process involving the contribution of formal and informal work experience. (Smith *et al.*, 1989, p. 3)

We explored the concept of *competence* at the beginning of Chapter 4. The term has been used by some commentators in a broad, all-encompassing sense. In the context of the debate surrounding management competence in Britain in the late 1980s, however, it became a label attached to highly fragmented dimensions of management activity. In order to differentiate the argument developed in this book from the current competency debate, we have found it useful to adopt the term *expertise* to include the diagnostic and judgemental capabilities of the change agent as well as the individual skills or competences that research has identified. The expertise of the change agent can thus be seen to consist of more than a collection of fragmented competences, and is also more than just the exercise of managerial judgement. This view has implications for approaches to the development of change management expertise; management expertise in general can also be considered in similar terms.

Cognitive psychology has developed a particular interest in the concept of expertise only since the mid-1980s, triggered by attempts to develop computer-based expert systems (sometimes also described as intelligent knowledge-based systems). The research tradition in psychology from which this work developed was previously dominated by concerns with the nature and acquisition of skill and with human problem solving, and chose comparatively well-bounded tasks and problems as the basis for empirical study and theory building. (The study of chess and the game's master players has, for example, been popular in this domain for some time.) Attention has now switched to the exploration of less well-bounded and 'knowledge-rich' tasks. This could also be expressed as a move from the study of well-defined problems with known solutions, to an exploration of situations where problem definition is itself problematic, and where different experts are likely to disagree on what constitutes a 'good' solution.

Methods for capturing and encoding the knowledge and decision processes of skilled performers are now relatively well developed in some spheres. Expert systems are thus beginning to impinge on management roles in specialized areas, particularly with respect to management decision support, but are more widely applied in other professional settings, such as medical diagnosis. The relevance of expert- and decision-support systems to management, given the current state of development of hardware and software, has been seriously challenged (Martin, 1988). Cognitive psychology has yet to extend the study of expertise to organizational change agents.

While it has not been directly concerned with the themes of this book, psychological research in the field of expertise has revealed some of the key characteristics of 'expert performance' which are relevant to our argument. Glaser and Chi (1988) summarize the main characteristics that have emerged from the research so far, pointing out that these characteristics apply across a wide range of different activity settings. The characteristics of expertise that they identify are:

---

1. Experts excel in their own domains

Those who are highly skilled in one activity or domain cannot always transfer that expertise to another domain. Expertise is often based on extensive *domain-specific* knowledge, often developed through long experience, and not on the global qualities of the individual's thought processes or intellect. Expert physicians are thus able to recognize many more variants of common diseases; expert taxi drivers know more short cuts to avoid traffic jams. The implication of this finding for our purposes is simply that managers who are technically proficient in their specialist domain – information technology or production management, for example – will not necessarily be proficient organizational change agents.

---

2. Experts work with large and meaningful patterns

Chess masters, research has revealed, do not store in memory information about individual pieces and moves, but instead recall *clusters* of the pieces that they see, or even whole sequences from previous games. In other words, they are able to organize the information available to them – what cognitive psychologists refer to as the 'knowledge base' – more effectively. This characteristic has been demonstrated with reading circuit diagrams, interpreting x-ray plates, reading architectural plans, and computer programming. This relates to our earlier comments about the need for the change agent to take a 'helicopter perspective' of the organization and the process of change, to climb above the fine detail and have a broad overview of events and issues.

---

3. Experts solve problems quicker and with less error

This is a straightforward observation, and there are at least two explanations for it. First, skill becomes automatic and thus faster with practice, particularly with simpler tasks, such as typing for example. Second, given the expert's attention to pattern rather than detail, solutions may be identified without extensive and time-consuming prior search. The perceived patterns themselves quickly trigger ideas for solutions and actions, reducing the need for detailed information gathering and analysis.

---

4. Experts have superior memories

This is presumably because the automatic nature of expert skill frees up memory space, and because the patterning or 'chunking' of information allows for more effective storage than if it were remembered detail by detail. Experts do not necessarily have larger memory capacity, they simply use what is available to them more efficiently. This finding seems to apply both to short-term and long-term memory.

---

5. Experts use deeper, more principled conceptualizations of problems

---

When novices and experts are asked to analyse and group problems, novices build categories around literal objects in the problem description, while experts use theoretical principles relevant to the problem domain. For example, when expert and novice programmers were asked to sort programming problems, experts sorted them according to solution algorithms, while novices sorted them with reference to their areas of application. The conceptual categories used by experts thus appear to be less superficial and more principle-based than those used by novices who tend to rely more on surface features. This proposition, from a different research tradition, supports the view of McCaskey (1988), explained in Chapter 2, that change agents working with unstructured problems require 'map-building' skills in generating appropriate conceptualizations of problem situations.

---

6. Experts spend more time qualitatively analysing problems

The research shows that while novices tend to plunge quickly into problem solving, experts tend to stand back and try to understand the problem first. This seems to involve building a mental representation of the problem from which to infer relationships and help to define the situation and its constraints. This does not contradict the previous point about the speed of the expert; experts can be slower than novices in the initial stages of problem solving, but still solve problems faster overall.

---

7. Experts have strong self-monitoring skills

Experts seem to be more aware when they have made an error, why they have not understood, and when they need to check their solutions. Experts tend to ask more questions, particularly with respect to difficult materials and issues. Self-knowledge also seems to give experts better ability to assess the difficulty of a situation facing them.

What are the implications of this analysis for the recruitment and selection of project managers, and for change management development? If we apply these conclusions to the role of change agent or project manager, the expert or ideal 'person specification' which emerges is an individual who:

- regards him-/herself primarily as a specialist in organizational change, and not necessarily as a technical or functional specialist, and has signficant aspirations and/or previous experience in the organizational change domain;
- is good at 'pattern detection' when faced with complex organizational settings, is able to rise above the detail, is able to take a broad overview of current events and future developments, is capable of adopting a 'helicopter perspective';
- does not waste much time in approaching his/her work, is good at defining problems and situations quickly, and at rapidly generating appropriate solutions once the problem has been understood;
- has a store of relevant experiences on which to draw and is able to relate those experiences effectively to current issues and problems;
- is good at conceptualizing complex organizational problems, and perhaps at simplifying them in the face of large amounts of information, and has good diagnostic and analytical skills;

- is good at organizing information to highlight key issues, at problem representation, and at 'map-building' with respect to problems and the implementation of appropriate solutions;
- is self-aware, self-critical, self-questioning, and information hungry.

Expertise thus seems to involve a combination of ability to organize and to process knowledge effectively, and is not simply based on the possession of superior knowledge. The development of expertise, given these seven characteristics, can clearly be assisted by formal training and educational processes. Conceptual skills, theoretical frameworks, problem-solving methodologies and self-awareness, can all be developed through instruction to improve self-monitoring, problem-analysis, and problem conceptualization skills. It can clearly be seen, however, that the mere possession of techniques in those areas is inadequate and that expertise must also be based on extensive domain experience; Glaser and Chi (1988, p. xxi) refer to 'knowledge-rich tasks – tasks that require hundreds and thousands of hours of learning and experience'. Michael Posner (1988) from a review of key research studies also points to the significance of exposure to large numbers of experiences in the development of expertise. Given the significance of time and experience, Posner adds that: 'The problem of producing an expert may be not so much in selecting someone who has special capability, but to create and maintain the motivation needed for long-continued training' (Posner, 1988, p. xxxv). The evidence seems to support the 'made, not born' argument for the development of expertise; innate ability alone is insufficient.

Organizational strategies for the development of expertise in change management clearly must take these findings into account. However, if expertise is so hard won, over protracted periods of experience and practice, can the process be speeded up in any way? The obvious answer is to identify the effective strategies used by acknowledged experts and to use these expert strategies as training tools. Staszewski (1988) offers research support for the view that the identification, description, evaluation and use of expert strategies as instructional tools can indeed be used to speed up the development process. His evidence comes from the domain of expert mental calculation, but there is no reason to suspect that this argument is not generally applicable.

We argued at the end of Chapter 4 that the expertise of the change agent lies in a combination of diagnostic and judgemental capabilities with specific management skills or competences. This view is broadly consistent with the conceptualization of expertise derived from cognitive psychology and from other domains of human activity. We can now be more specific about this concept of expertise as it applies to the organizational change agent, drawing together the various components of the argument developed throughout this book. The model that we have developed is outlined in Table 5.1.

Table 5.1 first summarizes the following five diagnostic areas that we have previously identified:

1. *Organizational type* The change agent requires the diagnostic skill to

determine organizational type, and how that type may be changing or need to be changed, along a continuum from rigid and mechanistic to fuzzy and organic. This is not a clear-cut distinction. Different sections of the same organization may display mechanistic and organic characteristics.

2. *Change category*   The change agent requires diagnostic skill to determine the nature of change in hand, in terms of the quadrant in our simple model to which it belongs, and also to determine how that categorization is or should be migrating through time. We identified quadrant four – radical change affecting the core of the business, also characterized by shifts in pace of change – as creating for the change agent the highest levels of hassle and vulnerability, and thus being the most demanding.

3. *Personal vulnerability*   The change agent requires diagnostic skill to assess personal vulnerability. This is likely to be higher in organic organizational settings, where change is radical and affects the core of the business, and where there are frequent shifts in goals and priorities, multiple interdependencies, uncertainty over management responsibility for change, and lack of clarity concerning the stance of senior management.

4. *Agenda priorities*   The change agent requires diagnostic skill to determine the relative priorities of the three agendas, concerning content, control and process. The process and control agendas are likely to assume high priority in high vulnerability settings, and the content and control agendas are likely to assume high priority in low vulnerability settings.

5. *Public performance and backstage activity*   The change agent requires diagnostic skill and judgement to determine how to construct the public performance of change in accordance with organizational expectations and how most effectively to support that performance with backstage activity. This involves a series of judgement calls, based on the change agent's knowledge and understanding of critical events in the organization's past which have coloured attitudes and expectations, and of current organizational norms and standards. There is considerable scope for innovation here with respect to the behaviour of the change agent in sustaining public performance with backstage activity; this is not a mechanical process in which actions are determined by and matched to the organizational context.

Presenting these dimensions of diagnosis in this manner may give the impression that we are dealing with a complex series of judgements based on sophisticated understanding. That is not necessarily the case. Reaching the appropriate diagnosis under each of these headings will in many instances be relatively straightforward, if not in some cases intuitively transparent to the change agent concerned. Table 2.1, which outlined the distinction between mechanistic and organic management sytems, can be used as a diagnostic guide in a particular organizational setting. Figure 2.1 can be used to locate the nature of the change proposals in terms of the hassle and personal vulnerability which the change agent can expect to face. Table 2.7 can be used more precisely to establish the degree and nature of the vulnerability facing the change agent given the characteristics of the context. It is helpful to be clear about the nature of the context in which one is operating when planning a change strategy and identifying specific tactics.

It is also necessary to reinforce the point that the competences which we have identified are likely to be ineffective in the absence of appropriate (albeit tacit or intuitive) diagnosis and judgement. Competence without diagnosis can lead to a lot of action without clear focus and direction. On the other hand, the exercise of diagnostic capability, however sophisticated, is likely to be equally ineffective in the absence of appropriate (albeit straightforward) management competences. Diagnosis without competence is likely to result in a lot of good planning with little activity.

Table 5.1 then summarizes the five competence clusters and fifteen specific elements identified in Chapter 4, concerning goals, roles, communication, negotiation, and managing up. Once again it it useful to point out that, despite the length of this list and the impression of offering the change agent a 'heavy tool-kit', these are well-understood general management skills and attributes.

Table 5.1 also summarizes the three dimensions of the process of change, concerning the 'unfolding logics' of problem solving, ownership and legitimation. The change agent's expertise in constructing a process in which these three logics are seen to unfold in the organization in an appropriate and acceptable manner thus influences the perceived personal effectiveness of the change agent, as well as the effectiveness of the change. Most prescriptive accounts of the change implementation process suggest the sequence of steps or phases which the change agent is advised to follow. In the perspective developed here, such advice is inappropriate. The phasing of change implementation – the overall strategy and detailed tactics – will depend on the context, and primarily on the organizational expectations concerning how the three logics should be seen to unfold.

The change agent's task is to construct the broad and detailed timing and sequencing of events with these outcomes in mind, and this does not necessarily involve following, even loosely, a predetermined set of stages. On the contrary, the social construction of the process of change, or what Kanter (1983) calls 'change architect skill', is a *creative* activity. Expertise does not simply involve the mechanical deployment of diagnostic tools, competences and stereotyped solutions, but involves also the innovative and opportunistic exploitation of other dimensions of the organizational context. An example from a different domain may help to illustrate this argument relating expertise and opportunism more effectively. From their study of expertise in the medical diagnosis of x-ray pictures, Lesgold *et al.* (1988) seek to demonstrate that:

Expert problem-solving capability is opportunistic. That is, it takes account of new possibilities when they arise. With some forms of expertise, opportunism is easily apparent. For example, an expert quarterback, seeing a hole in the defensive line, will run through it even if he had been planning a slightly different play. In the case of diagnosis, opportunism is less obvious. After all,

Table 5.1   The expertise of the change agent

Diagnostics	Competences	Process outcomes	Personal and organizational outcomes
1. Organization type	Goals 1. Sensitivity	• The logic of problem solving	• Perceived organizational effectiveness
2. Change category	2. Clarity	• The logic of ownership	• Positive evaluation of change
3. Personal vulnerability	3. Flexibility	• The logic of legitimacy	
4. Agenda priorities	Roles 4. Team building		• Perceived personal effectiveness
5. Public performance and backstage activity	5. Networking 6. Tolerance of ambiguity		• Positive evaluation of personal credibility
	Communication 7. Communication 8. Interpersonal skills 9. Personal enthusiasm 10. Stimulating motivation		
	Negotiation 11. Selling 12. Negotiating		
	Managing up 13. Political awareness 14. Influencing 15. Helicopter perspective		

the patient is there, the physician has the data, and it doesn't seem as if any new opportunities will arise. However, there is still room for two types of opportunism. First, it is possible that new data will be obtained, such as lab reports that appear from time to time. Second, the noticing of features takes time, and it is possible that a newly noticed feature may represent an opportunity to view the case from a different perspective. Both forms of opportunity seem to be used to greater advantage by experts. (Lesgold *et al.*, 1988, p. 332)

It is an intuitively appealing proposition that the effective organizational change agent is creative and opportunistic in collecting and using new information, and in developing new perspectives on which to base management action. However, further research will be required to document this aspect of change management behaviour adequately in the interests either of theoretical advance or management development.

The advice on offer from this perspective is, however, designed to assist the change agent in framing the implementation sequence in a manner appropriate to the objectives of change and the context in which it is set. We have sought to develop understanding of the change implementation process, and to identify the tools that can be used in that process. There are many different ways to deploy those tools, and this is a matter of creative, non-mechanical choice and judgement, taking into account the contingencies in the context. This also involves a careful consideration of what behaviour – particularly backstage activity – is ethical and acceptable, given the organizational culture and circumstances, as we discussed in Chapter 3. As in most other areas of management, there is no 'one best way'.

Backstaging in action

The audio diary data afford a number of illustrative examples of backstage activity. The small sample inevitably means that these diary entries offer only partial coverage of the range of activity under this heading, but they are offered here in order to provide a flavour of what is involved in practice, in the words of the diarists themselves.

This diary entry, for example, deals with an aspect of managing up with respect to developing and exploiting personal relationships to help sell plans and ideas to other senior management:

My role at the moment as advisor to the senior management group means I am not actually a part of that group and therefore not involved on all issues, therefore difficult with something like this which will affect that group perhaps to get a hearing for it. That's something I'll look at. Also concerned about relations back to individuals who make up the group. Perhaps need to identify someone within that senior group to talk the issues through and will take them forward or help me to take them forward. (Chief Officer, probation service)

This diary entry describes how perceptions can be influenced through the deliberate witholding of information from the senior management team:

In this respect it was apparent to me that [the Managing Director] did not communicate the main issues which arose during the course of the project to his Board. For example, when we reviewed the capital requirements with the contractor, it was some weeks later that I discovered that the rest of the Board had not been told of our decision to reduce capacity in order to reduce capital cost. (Engineering Director, oil refining)

Building a coalition, recruiting support, establishing legitimacy for plans and ideas are all 'power skills' in Rosabeth Moss Kanter's terms. Often in the early stages of a change project, this kind of backstage activity is required simply to generate momentum behind the ideas. This can be a very time-consuming activity, and again involves a lot of face-to-face activity and the use of personal relationships to build agreement and commitment, as these diary entries illustrate:

Over the last year my part-time team had done a lot of work with each of their own plant staffs to convince them of the need for investment in order fulfilment and order scheduling in particular. My European functional boss had also been doing work with the European management team to convince them of the need for major investment in this area . . . . My functional boss and I therefore spent many long hours putting together an overall picture of how our order fulfilment systems could look in four years' time and what would need to be done next year and the year after that in order to get there. This was the culmination of about fifteen months of part-time work, with the best brains we have available, who understand the front end of our business, to try and get our own corporation to move forward. I think the text books would probably call them 'change agents'. Basically we had been boot-legging for fifteen months across all our European sites, getting people's time, people's money, to try and put a plan and a package together that we could go away and work on to develop a new solution. We were now at the point where we needed some more legitimacy.

Let me summarize the actions that I have taken in order to rectify these three situations. Let's deal with V representation first. Basically what I have had to do is speak to the individual himself who I know well from the past is making a very clear statement around availability. I understand the circumstances in V, having worked there for some time and therefore with the individual. I have agreed that we will put together a plan to augment the materials and planning resource in V. I will take that plan to the manager in V and also the group manager in A and try to provide the support required in order that we can do the programme in V, but also support this longer-term programme. (Business Manager, computer manufacturing)

Backstage activity can also relate to the way in which investment decisions and their justifications are presented. The public face can sometimes conceal other lines of reasoning, for example in protecting individuals from the possible negative outcomes of incorrect decisions, as these two diary entries explain:

The next major decision point was to follow the parent company in obtaining a more sophisticated computer aided design system. This last decision has changed the direction of implementation of our new technology. Outwardly, it was made as an opportunistic decision though inwardly it was clearly hoped by many of those involved on both sides of the Atlantic that this would be of significant strategic importance with the cost justification not being as clear as in previous cases. From the UK point of view the decision to follow the American parent company was basically a low risk decision since it was not clearly stated but it was obviously hoped by one or more of the people involved in the decision that if anything should go wrong with the decision the blame could be placed squarely on the shoulders of those who had made the decision in the USA.

Use of a computer programme to calculate internal rate of return on discounted cash flow helped considerably enabling 'what if' calculations to be made. It was therefore possible to project that the increasing work load of the company anticipated in three years would require the employment of a new draughtsman. This employment could be avoided by the installation of computer aided design equipment. It was considered that this was a low risk justification and would be difficult to prove correct or otherwise. (Technical Director, engineering company)

The timing and location of events in the change implementation process can clearly influence perceptions, particularly where prior events can be used in support of subsequent actions. This diary entry describes how change implementation was deliberately phased to target potential opposition groups only once firm evidence of the benefits had been demonstrated elsewhere in the organization (although the 'public' explanation within the organization for this sequence of events was couched in other terms):

There were some cases of resistance to change and instances of protectionism. This had a direct effect on how, when and where the project should progress. We implemented in the areas where we had total support so that when we reached the areas where we were expecting opposition, we had proved our point and we were able to display examples of our success. (Management Services Manager, local authority)

Peter Keen (1981) argues that the change agent should rely on face-to-face interaction to sell, influence and otherwise persuade other members of the organization to accept change. This diary entry offers a further illustration of such backstage activity:

So therefore I decided that it was important to communicate with area managers, talk about the system, talk about what the objectives are, and really to, more or less, not perhaps get them on my side but to impart a fuller understanding that the system is really not intended to spy on them in any way, but is intended to help them to improve their performance and also the department's performance. (Systems Manager, public utility)

Andrew Pettigrew (1985) and Rosabeth Moss Kanter (1983) both recommend the creative use of staff appointments and movements to encourage change. These diary entries illustrate such steps:

As the system progressed, the middle management role of the design manager became more difficult. The engineers themselves were concerned with the future, were frustrated with system inadequacies, and the cell development task did not utilize their skills or knowledge. The manager's role, therefore, was concerned with day-to-day motivation. It was at this stage that the manager began to review the situation with a view to moving some engineers into other groups and altering the staff to obtain people suitable to the expected future roles.

Negotiation, counselling and employee development skills were all deployed. First, the manager used his judgement to move staff into other functions in order to keep talented people within the company. The staff involved were given the opportunity to discuss the move and all those approached supported the transfers enthusiastically. It was agreed, of course, that this move would be viewed negatively by some remaining members of the group. The manager, however, decided that the welfare of the majority was most important and considered other ways which would help the section head during this difficult period. (Logic Manager, electronics manufacturing)

Confidence in management decisions can be based on information collection and analysis. It can also be improved through special relationships which individuals can use to check and reinforce their thinking, as this diary entry shows:

My involvement was really in the role of right-hand man to answer queries, to provide support, to go along to meetings and to assist the Managing

Director through these meetings and generally to help where there was any confusion and to smooth the way – to let the MD feel that at least the decisions he had made had been clearly thought through. I became a sort of sounding board to shoot off ideas or to widen his view. (Director, land survey company)

Backstage activity pervades the change implementation process. These examples illustrate some of the characteristics of such activity, which was explored in more depth in Chapter 3. These diary entries thus offer a partial picture of this aspect of change management, from the perspective of the change agent directly involved in the process.

From the perspective of the technical or functional specialist, we are dealing here with what are often labelled as 'soft' skills or competences. Communication, negotiation, motivation, conflict resolution and so on are often seen as intangible, invisible and unquantifiable abilities. They are in many organizational settings undervalued and can go unrewarded. Backstage activities similarly lack the benefits of public visibility and can receive similarly dismissive treatment, but are critical nevertheless.

Given the potential intangibility of backstage activities, and the partial and selective nature of our diary illustrations, it may be useful to provide a summary of these techniques in a prescriptive mode, and to bring together material that we have introduced at various points earlier in the text, mainly in Chapter 3. In doing this, we move beyond the generalized accounts we have offered so far, and address directly the change agent seeking advice on how to achieve certain ends and resolve particular problems, concentrating on the use of backstaging techniques. Typical issues in this respect, from our experience, amenable to at least partial attack through backstage activities, can include the following:

- How to get action from a senior manager who has given agreement, but who will not do anything practical, public or visible about it.
- How to reconcile actual resource requirements with senior management expectations.
- How to get the willing cooperation of other people, sections and functions at critical stages during implementation.
- How to get those who are making unreasonable demands or requests to back off – tactfully.
- How to avoid or to deal appropriately with other activities – whether urgent or trivial – that will delay progress by diverting staff energies and other resources in other directions.

It should be clear that each of these problems can have a range of possible solutions, given the context in which it is set. The 'correct answer' depends on the creativity and judgement of the change agent in that particular setting. There is no 'one best way' or quick fix for dealing with issues like these. The action most likely to be effective will be, as we have sought to emphasize, dependent on current and past aspects of the organizational context. A combination of public and backstage activities will be appropriate in most settings, and it is not the intention to imply here that backstaging is a panacea.

The backstaging techniques which we have identified seem to fall into three broad categories, concerning ways of manipulating *structures*, manipulating *relationships*, and manipulating *language*. What follows is less a practical checklist and more an illustration of 'things to try' in addressing change implementation problems. These are some of the main backstage 'wheels and levers'. This prescriptive advice is offered, therefore, as a summary of creative and practical ideas and not as a definitive guide.

Manipulating structures

---

1. Remember that people are most likely to resist changes which adversely affect their access to information, and their responsibility, influence, autonomy and power base in the organization. Introduce changes to structures in ways that minimize these power and influence implications, or that offer other opportunities and trade-offs for potential losers, or that render ineffective the protestations and the power and influence bases of the losers. You always have a range of options with respect to organization structures. Assess and use the options.

2. Alter aspects of the organization structure in ways that are indirectly related to the changes to be introduced, but which reinforce and support them. Directly relevant structural alterations may be too obvious and attract immediate and unwelcome resistance. Close down sections of the organization, move people, and create new and perhaps *ad hoc* structures to help with the process of shifting current thought patterns. Design new management development policies and programmes as vehicles for introducing new ways of thinking and acting. Such changes may be substantive, but can also have powerful symbolic value in fostering a climate of change, and in fostering the desired changes – and thus increasing receptivity to further change. The broad aim with such approaches is to get people worried – to foster the concern that the status quo is no longer effective or appropriate. Judgement is required here; if used inappropriately and in the wrong context, deliberately induced flux can induce resistance to further change.

3. Others ways of fostering a climate of change and adaptation include setting up special steering committees or task forces or business teams, commissioning research and reports, and hiring outside consultants (who may even be briefed in advance on the anticipated contents and conclusions of their report). External recommendation and sanction can sometimes be more powerful than internal argument. Researched conclusions can be more

powerful than personal opinions. In short, 'they say we should do this', or 'the evidence says we should do this', is more powerful than 'I say we should do this'.

4. Reward new and desired behaviours by adjusting payment systems, by subtle shifts in promotion policy, and by creating new career paths which are, of course, seen to favour and promote those who are clearly behind the changes. The appropriate promotions of key (supporting) individuals can also help to reinforce these other symbolic moves through changing perceptions of self-interest (i.e. by changing what people have to be seen to be doing to get promoted around here). This has to be achieved in such a way that those who are thus favoured are seen to be making other substantive contributions which merit reward and are not promoted merely for their agreement with a particular policy. However, it is important that everybody else knows that those who are favoured do support that policy.

5. Form task forces and project teams around specific issues and particular problems. These may be *ad hoc*, and generate reports and analyses that promote change in the desired directions. The public agenda of the task force may be to conduct a feasibility study; the backstage agenda is to generate evidence supporting and justifying the proposed changes. Appoint 'co-ordinators', or coordinating committees to handle contentious issues and deal with contentious decisions.

6. Make the *ad hoc* arrangements formal when appropriate by adding them to the organization chart. Have public displays to welcome the new structures. Celebrate the appointment of new personnel to key positions. Send signals through such symbolic actions that these changes are not reversible.

7. The timing of structural changes is often significant. You may have to wait until someone leaves or retires or is 'creatively promoted' to another part of the organization. These creative departures are, of course, then replaced by known supporters of the changes.

Manipulating relationships

---

1. Get a senior manager or managers to support, or at least to say that they sanction, some main dimension of the change or changes. Attach at least one senior and powerful figure to the proposals; recruit influential friends and colleagues to the steering group or task force. The sponsorship of senior and respected figures is critical.

2. Tell those who would block your proposals that senior managers are on your side and that in challenging you they are challenging them. And remind them if appropriate when their next performance appraisal and salary review are scheduled and who will be conducting these.

3. Make sure that, at key meetings, your backers and supporters are not only

present but that they make all the right noises at all the right times, particularly in the face of counter-implementation and other resistance. You will invariably need to brief your backers informally and in advance of such confrontations to avoid inconsistencies in language and approach in the formal meeting. You may need to set aside a budget for time, lunches and dinners for these informal briefings.

4. Find ways of involving those to be affected in ways that they will perceive to be meaningful and give them feelings of ownership. Do not disclose your own thinking in detail. Instead, set the general directions and let the specific ideas and solutions that you favour emerge naturally in the course of participation so that those who make the suggestions feel that they have made their own personal contributions. Get people – even potential resistors – involved in information gathering, analysis and diagnosis.

5. How good are your interpersonal relationships with those who are blocking or who might block your proposals? Can you invite them to join the task force, get them involved, find out more about and try to meet their objections, and win them round this way? Be seen to understand the arguments of opponents and address them.

6. Challenge existing arrangements and views, encourage conflict and dissent, and facilitate argument and debate. In colloquial terminology, stir it up. Allow such arguments to surface. These symbolic actions help to generate and reinforce the climate of change by encouraging others to begin to think differently.

7. Use your own sense of humour, enthusiasm, confidence and commitment to 'infect' and therefore to stimulate others. You may need to display these attributes even when progress is poor and you are personally not at all amused, confident and enthusiastic about the way things are going. However, if you are driving change and if you are also seen to be depressed and miserable about it, this will have a predictable effect on the energy and enthusiasm levels of those around you.

8. Choose a 'well-connected' team of people to work with, people with good appropriate contacts inside and outside the organization. This formal and informal network is a source of information and ideas, and can also be called upon to exert interpersonal pressures in certain circumstances. If you cannot persuade a key individual or group, can you get someone else in the network, with the right relationship and credibility, to do this for you? The recipient of the influence attempt does not need to know, of course, that you have 'set up' the person or people exerting such persuasion. This should simply involve someone that they know well and respect.

9. Work with *ad hoc* or temporary project teams and task forces where appropriate. Make sure that your membership includes people whose credibility and integrity are widely known and respected, whose views will be seen to 'carry weight' around other sections of the organization.

10. Encourage those who actively support the initiative to take appropriate steps

to implement initial changes, without necessarily committing the organization to a larger-scale programme. Smaller-scale premilinary steps may not even be related in the perceptions of others to the more ambitious plans that have not yet been fully revealed. You can in this case also point to the lack of personal involvement in what is happening, because these initial steps are being implemented by someone else.

11. Give subordinates projects and reports to prepare, the outcomes of which can be used systematically and selectively to support the options you favour and to discredit other options. You will not then be seen to be producing the evidence on which proposals are selected and pursued. You can refer instead, objectively, to the results of studies and analyses carried out by others without visible personal intervention. Immediately highlight, publicize and widely comment on and praise the findings and the people that support the changes you favour. You can omit to take such actions with respect to the other reports – which, of course, you want a colleague to digest and comment on first, which require further analysis, need more time to read and absorb properly, are awaiting confirming results, and so on.

12. Adopt the role of fixer/facilitator. Rely on personal, face-to-face contact and communication rather than on written communications, large meetings, and third-party intermediaries. Personal persuasion and influence is always more powerful; at least you took the trouble to go meet and talk with somebody.

Manipulating language

---

1. Remembering the importance of ritual in establishing legitimacy and credibility, frame your proposals for change in a format that approximates the rational-linear model of the change implementation or project life cycle – identify problem, generate solutions, choose best solution, implement, review. Make it look as though change implementation will follow, or is following these logical steps. This generates confidence in the belief that 'things are being done properly'. Maintain the appearance of rationality. Maintain your own professional image and integrity in this way.

2. Look at the length and variety of the current agenda for changes in the organization. Do your proposals stand out as significant, or will they be competing with a range of other pressing items? Can you move your proposals onto that list at this time or should you wait? Can your proposals subsume any of the other, otherwise competing, items on that list? Can you challenge any of the items on the agenda to have them removed?

3. Word proposals for change in such a way that they can be seen to fit with current values and ideals. They are more difficult to challenge if they fit like this.

4. Arguments and justifications must use language that is acceptable in the

organization culture and that will be attractive to and not offend relevant senior managers. Communications may need to be 'personalized' with respect to particular managers or management groups to get the necessary agreement. This will involve a knowledge of individual beliefs, hostilities, aspirations and expectations. Proposals phrased and justified in one format could be quite acceptable, while phrased differently with other arguments in support will be rejected out of hand. This is not uncommon. Do your homework on your 'targets', if you do not already know them well.

5. Make appeals to opportunities and threats generated outside the organization to justify change proposals. Exploit, create or even invent a crisis if necessary. Such arguments are more powerful and acceptable, usually, than arguments based on personal aspirations or on departmental empire building (although those motives may also be relevant). Note that the created or invented crisis has to materialize sooner or later or you will lose credibility. One strategy for achieving this is to bring a crisis back in time; 'we won't hit this for another two years, but it will take us at least two years to get our planning and our new systems together, so we had better act now!'

6. It hardly needs stating that you need to consider carefully the social and organizational forums in which you express the private motives behind change in private language. However, it can be damaging to deny such private motives; altruism attracts suspicion in our culture. Private motives are understood to be a source of drive, energy and ambition and as such are perceived as legitimate – expressed in the right context.

7. Single communication and single persuasion or influence attempts are rarely successful. Repeat your message and your arguments; be persistent; and although such repetition may appear redundant, it can keep the issue 'live' as well as reinforcing the points you want people to have in front of them.

8. Make proposals more significant by describing them as vital to organizational survival, competitiveness or profitability. Relate proposals to pressing concerns and crises to make them more immediate and to trigger quicker action. Encourage the general impression that change is required; create the 'felt need'.

9. Make proposals more acceptable and understandable by making them more specific and focused – by grounding them in immediate realities – if abstractness is a barrier to broader acceptance and understanding.

10. Make proposals wider and more generally applicable – by clouding them with abstractions – if specificity is a barrier to broader acceptance across the organization. As a general rule, however, vague and abstract goals can become too complex to attract committed support. People need to have a clear idea of what they are being asked to buy into. The appropriate degrees of specificity and abstraction in change proposals are therefore a matter of judgement. Some dimensions may be more appropriately expressed in detailed terms, while others may be more appropriately left expressed as generalities, perhaps until a later time.

11. State proposals in simpler terms if complexity is a barrier to comprehension and acceptability. Relate proposals to other issues and dimensions if simplicity and narrowness of focus is a barrier to acceptance. This again is clearly a matter of judgement and timing.

12. Increase the acceptability of your proposals by expressing them where possible in ways that make them seem challenging and interesting while at the same time safe and uncontentious. Word proposals so that they appear to be trial-able, reversible, divisible, concrete, familiar, congruent with current arrangements, and have publicity value. Anticipate the likely resistance and word proposals in such a way that counter-arguments are disarmed before they are expressed (although you cannot expect this approach simply and alone to overcome all resistance).

13. Increase the acceptability of your proposals by presenting them in a manner that makes them appear to be phased in a straightforward and simple sequence – which preferably follows organizational custom and ritual and approximates a rational model of change implementation. The actual phasing may in reality be quite different, but is generally unclear and confused enough to permit the future unfolding of events to be articulated in this way, and to allow the past unfolding of those events to be reconstructed in this logical manner.

14. Choose words that mean action and avoid words that mean delay. Increase the acceptability of your proposals by expressing them in positive results-oriented language. This means using terms such as 'cut', 'eliminate', 'improve', 'remove', 'grow', and 'challenge'. Do not use language that implies further study and analysis such as 'review', 'study', 'define', 'monitor', 'explore' and 'investigate'. Such terms imply procrastination because more homework has still to be done before proposals can be finalized. Such language can therefore give others excuse for delay.

We suggested that this should be seen as a checklist of 'wheels and levers' to turn and throw to achieve progress in the face of change implementation problems. Used with tact in context, these approaches in combination with each other and with conventional project management tools can be highly effective. Used cynically out of context, these approaches clearly will fail. To demonstrate how this advice can potentially be used as a source of creative ideas, let us return to one of the typical problems raised at the beginning of this prescriptive section:

How do you get action from a senior manager who has given agreement, but who will not do anything practical, public or visible about it?

Working through the three broad areas of backstaging, the following possibilities emerge. Will the proposed changes threaten in some respect the status of the manager concerned and can this dimension of the proposal be dropped or amended? Can you at least persuade the manager to sanction the formation of a task force with a budget, with some executive power and with a nominated leader who can then act without further reference? You may need to write the memo which your manager then signs. Can you get agreement to proceed with one key preliminary aspect of the overall plan, pointing out of course that this does not commit the organization to the whole scheme? Maybe you will just have to wait until this manager retires, leaves, is promoted, or goes on an extended business development tour of the Pacific Rim – and you can take it up with whoever deputizes.

Can you get another senior manager of comparable or higher rank to sanction progress? Can you get that other senior manager to do some arm twisting to get the action you now need? Is there another even more senior manager to whom you can appropriately address an appeal? Can you and your colleagues confront your manager as a united group, demonstrating mass support behind a plan that only one individual is now holding up? Can you get a colleague or a subordinate to implement partial and apparently unrelated changes so that you can begin to document and demonstrate some of the benefits of going ahead with a fully developed proposal? What evidence is there from other experience, research and analyses that you can present in support – from internal and external sources?

Maybe you worded the proposal in a way that was seen by the senior manager concerned as inappropriate and damaging and that you do not yet know about? Can you check this? Are other priorities making demands on time, energy, staff and money, pushing your proposals down the list of actions that are currently grabbing management attention? You could then consider ways of enhancing the significance of your proposals in an attempt to change the relative priorities. Was your justification dependent on technical criteria, or are you able to point to external opportunities and threats to get faster movement? Are the required action steps explained and phased clearly enough, or are these aspects too vague? Finally, do not overlook the impact of persistence. Just because an approach has not worked yet, this does not necessarily mean that you can give it up. Keep pushing.

The approach or combination of approaches that works in resolving this particular problem will be dependent on the organizational context. These suggestions are offered as illustrations only.

Developing the expertise: an action-learning model

Our model of the expertise of the change agent thus comprises understanding of the nature of the process, diagnostic skills, and managerial judgement, and a number of specific competences. How can this expertise best be developed?

Conventional classroom-based approaches to management training and development can clearly contribute in this area, but that contribution must be limited, given in particular the nature of the diagnostic and judgemental capabilities involved. *Experiential learning* is therefore critical, used *in combination* with more or less conventional approaches.

Quinn *et al.* (1990) identify eight key management and leadership roles, each of which is associated with three competences, giving twenty-four management competences in all. They are concerned with management skills in general, and not exclusively with change management. However, one of the eight roles they identify is described as the 'innovator role', which involves the three competences of living with change, creative thinking, and managing change. They offer a five-step model for the development of these competences, and they label this the ALAPA approach because it comprises the following steps:

Step 1 Assessment
In which the individual discovers his/her current levels of ability in and awareness of each dimension of competence, through the use of questionnaires, role plays, and group discussion.

Step 2 Learning
In which knowledge is acquired through reading and presentations, through books and lectures, and through sharing of experience with colleagues and instructors.

Step 3 Analysis
Appropriate and inappropriate behaviours are explored through example in other typical situations, using case studies, role plays, and other forms of behaviour sampling.

Step 4 Practice
Competences are applied to a 'worklike situation' in the classroom, to provide opportunities for experimentation and for feedback.

Step 5 Application
The process is finally transferred to real-life situations, perhaps through assignments.

This is presented in the form of an approach to individual development, relying in the initial stages on more or less conventional classroom exercises to establish strengths and weaknesses, and to develop particular skills. ALAPA is thus a general systematic model for the development of a wide range of management capabilities, and does not focus on the needs of the change agent. The competences and their development are also presented in a context-free manner, contrary to the argument developed in this text.

Boddy and Buchanan (1987) offer an account of an action-learning programme, initially designed for information technology project managers, but subsequently used in an altered format for change agents working on other kinds of projects. This project combined conventional input, with an action-learning format, incorporating social support and challenge for those involved. This action-learning programme had the following features.

First, the number of participants was restricted to twelve, and only managers with current project responsibility were invited to join. Although from different (non-competing) organizations and sectors, the participant group thus shared common interests, concerns, pressures and problems with respect to the 'live' management of change. This was not a programme for those merely interested in change management, and it was important that participants came willing to share and to discuss their personal experiences.

Second, the programme met monthly, with nine meetings across a calendar year (with gaps for holiday periods). Each meeting was scheduled for a whole day. A small number of participants travelled significant distances and were unwilling to do so for shorter sessions; all participants valued the whole-day meeting format and this was reinforced in the programme evaluation, described below. It was important to leave the month-long gap between meetings to allow events to unfold in the life of the projects represented on the programme, to allow participants' thinking to evolve, to allow evaluation to take place, and to generate fresh analysis and discussion.

Third, the programme for each meeting combined the following aspects:

- Conventional input, drawn from a menu compiled and reviewed monthly by the instructors/facilitators in collaboration with the participants.
- Syndicate work on specific issues of interest and concern, with feedback of results to the group as a whole.
- Action-planning sessions, in which individual action plans from the previous meeting were reviewed, and in which action plans for the immediate future were prepared and exposed to syndicate group scrutiny and challenge.

This mixed format allowed for the sharing of experience, problems and progress. It also gave participants an opportunity to test ideas and plans on a 'neutral' audience, and to get advice, comments, questions and criticisms from other members of the group. Participants accepted a 'self-disclosure contract' with their syndicate group on the programme to reveal forward action plans at each meeting and to share progress (including difficulties) with the group at each subsequent meeting. This kind of planning and ideas check, with critical and constructive feedback, is rarely available within the base organization – or it can be difficult to find the people and the time to stage such events. This critical part of the process enabled participants, where appropriate, to adjust and improve their thinking and action plans before implementing them, or simply reinforced planning which had already been well-developed – and from which others could borrow ideas.

Input was to be provided by the instructors/facilitators. However, individual participants also contributed where they had specific experience and expertise relevant to the rest of the group. Participating companies allowed other senior managers to offer presentations to the group as a whole on key issues of common interest. Two meetings were hosted by participating companies. Participants also made their own personal side-deals to visit each other's sites, simply to observe, and to meet with other managers and technical staff where appropriate.

The ten key ingredients of an action-learning programme for change agents are as follows.

1. Varied participant group.
2. Restricted numbers.
3. Restricted participation: current project-based.
4. Monthly one-day meetings over a year.
5. Mixed programme of input and action planning.
6. Self-disclosure contract with syndicate.
7. Opportunity to present plans and ideas for feedback and constructive criticism.
8. Participants as presenters.
9. Company speakers.
10. Side-deals on site visits.

There can be a number of variants. For example, participants could be drawn from the separate divisions of one larger organization. The sharing of diverse experience across different sectors is valuable, but this can often be found within one large divisionalized company. On the programme described by Boddy and Buchanan (1987), some of the participating organizations nominated two representatives, at least one of whom attended each meeting, but frequently both were able to join. The syndicate groups within the programme were initially determined by participants on common interest criteria, but were reformed during the programme as those interests changed, and as access to a wider cross-section of experience became more highly valued.

This type of programme thus offers a rich and flexible mutual learning context for all those involved, not least the organizers. The approach blurs the distinctions between training, education and development as defined in the quote at the beginning of this chapter, by potentially combining aspects of all three into the programme. Development of appropriate skills, knowledge, diagnostic and judgemental capabilities, and competences thus takes place within the context of the participants' ongoing change implementation activities, not in a sterile academic or management training vacuum. Participants and their organizations are, however, asked to make a significant investment, in terms of the opportunity costs of management time, and also in terms of the costs involved in mounting a nine- to twelve-day programme across a year (although in this latter respect, the costs are spread).

Boddy and Buchanan (1987) carried out a systematic evaluation of their programme, and this produced the following four main findings:

1. *Participation was sustained* over the programme. A high drop-out rate was

anticipated, but nine of the twelve organizations represented at the first programme meeting were also represented at the last.
2. The first main benefit identified by participants was simply the opportunity for regular *time out*, away from the office pressures and interruptions, to reflect on and to clarify their thinking, their experience and their future plans.
3. The second main benefit identified by participants was the regular and structured opportunity for the *shared experience* of problems and solutions with managers from different organizations, but with similar responsibilities and experiences.
4. A third benefit identified by participants was the *growth in confidence* in individual project plans.

In developing the expertise required by the change agent, this action learning format combines the advantages of more or less conventional off-the-job training programmes with systematic experiential learning, based on current management activities and responsibilities and in relation to active change implementation projects. The formation of the participant group is therefore critical, to establish an appropriate context for the sharing of relevant experience, and the timing of meetings is also critical, to allow for the unfolding of events and for the development of participants' thinking and planning. Monthly sounds about right, but more or less frequent meetings could be more or less useful to particular participant groups given their special needs and circumstances.

The individual development process can be supported by systematic career planning that identifies and responds to the need to move project managers through organizational roles in which they are exposed to low and high vulnerability contexts as appropriate. Exposure to the issues can thus be linked to identification and development of the competences of the effective change agent. Selective, planned placement, rotation and exposure can thus play a key change agent or project management development function.

Roy Towndrow (1989), general manager of customer training at ICL, describes how his company's 'core training programme' takes managers from different parts of the company, and from different countries, through four development modules. The emphasis of the programme is on corporate strategy, market position, organization structure and self-assessment. The aim of the programme, which was judged successful, has been to improve individual and corporate ability to manage change. This is an interesting illustration of the need to develop approaches to individual management development that are linked to organizational goals, needs and strategies.

The research agenda

The argument presented in this text contains a number of gaps, and there are a number of remaining research needs in this area. Some of these issues concern change management processes, and some concern the development of appropriate expertise.

There are at least four interesting research areas which merit further investigation.

First, Andrew Pettigrew (1987) has proposed a challenging research agenda concerning the 'processual dynamics of changing', taking into account political, cultural and historical dimensions in addition to the other organizational and management issues explored in this book. Although complex, multi-layered and multivariate, Pettigrew's argument is compelling, and is likely to continue to influence studies of change for some time. Longitudinal research in particular is underrepresented in the organization theory and behaviour literature. Such research is difficult to sustain, as personnel in host and research organizations change, lose interest, or simply come under pressure to divert their attention to other issues. However, Pettigrew (1985) shows that this type of work can be sustained, and also demonstrates the benefits. More researchers need to accept this challenge.

Second, while we have highlighted the significance of backstage, ritual and symbolic action in change implementation, and while we have identified a number of sources where this type of prescription is available, this is also an underresearched topic. Johnson (1990) in particular makes a plea for further systematic investigation of this theme, which again can be inherently awkward by virtue of the nature of the behaviours being explored. Organizations and their members perhaps need to be persuaded of the benefits of allowing management researchers to investigate these issues openly, albeit confidentially and anonymously. More sophisticated 'conceptual maps' of this area are required to assist understanding, and from a management development perspective, further fine-grain empirical work would be useful in generating case studies and other illustrative materials for use in educational and training contexts.

Third, we have not in this account found space to deal with factors contributing to the success of change in any particular sector or with respect to specific types of technical or organizational change. With respect to the adoption and use of advanced manufacturing technology, Chris Voss (1988) makes a plea to raise the issue of implementation to a special field of study, overlooked in the past in this particular domain. He offers for further development a model of the implementation process which proceeds from antecedents, through pre-implementation to installation and post-commissioning. This is consistent with Pettigrew's request for an approach that deals with contextual, processual and historical issues, and Voss provides a structured framework on which to base such research. There may also be differential success factors across different industry sectors, and across changes different in content. Cultural differences in the management of change implementation offer a further fascinating field of future investigation.

Fourth, we have been using the term 'effective' throughout this book in a taken-for-granted manner. However, how should the effectiveness or success of change be evaluated? Voss (1988) distinguishes between technical success and business success. But when one considers the multiple stakeholders concerned with significant organizational changes, the criteria on which effectiveness can and should be rated become less clear. Establishing the multiple criteria of assessment, the mechanism of measurement, who will carry this out, and when and how often, all become problematic. Carnall (1990) offers a checklist with thirty-two dimensions on which change effectiveness can be assessed, sectioned into five areas concerning people, finance, marketing, operations, and business development. This is a useful general purpose tool for management development applications, and for monitoring in particular circumstances. The research task, however, is to establish the linkages between the conduct of the change implementation process and measures of effectiveness, so that we are in a better position to *explain* the success or failure of change on given criteria with reference to context and process and to the expertise of the change agent.

There are at least two management development issues that will repay further studies.

First, while action learning has become a well-established management development approach, and while the action-learning format specified here has been used with some success, further study is required to reveal the mechanisms through which the diagnostic and judgemental capabilities identified can best be developed. We have comparatively successful techniques for developing management competences, particularly in the social and interpersonal domains. Many management training programmes seem to assume, however, that providing the tools is enough to ensure their appropriate use. That is not necessarily the case. Our understanding of the diagnostic and judgemental skills that contribute to management expertise is weak, and it could be argued that this area is weakened further by the contemporary preoccupation with the assessment of fragmented competences. Action learning appears to be a more or less appropriate vehicle for developing such skills, but until we fully understand why this is so, it will be difficult to develop suitable approaches beyond that format. Action learning is a combination of approaches and establishing causal links will be awkward. Focused research into specific dimensions of management expertise, such as aspects of change management, and specific management development strategies, could prove valuable here.

Second, there remains the issue of assessment, of competence or of expertise. Developments have taken place in this area recently, thanks to the Management Charter Initiative which has consistently emphasized assessment of management performance as a key aim. University-style examinations have a poor reputation as valid and reliable assessment methods for managers in general, and MCI has encouraged the introduction of other practice-related approaches. MCI has in addition pressed for action on the accreditation of prior learning (APL), through which managers without conventional educational achievements to prove their worth can aspire to the award of nationally recognized qualifications by demonstrating their competence at work by other means. This is achieved mainly through the compilation of a portfolio representing activities undertaken and management successes achieved, prepared with the collaboration and help of a diagnostic APL assessor. The portfolio may contain a series of reports, projects and special assignments, testimonials and other relevant documentation, and may be supplemented by interviews and by management exercises, designed to display specific competences in the presence of observers-assessors. Clearly the assessors have to be specially and carefully trained to perform this delicate function, and the process can be extremely time consuming and expensive. These techniques are explained by Conway and Powney (1990) who note that a number of managers on a recent pilot APL scheme became so frustrated with the time involved that they moved on to a traditionally run certification programme instead. It seems likely that these problems will be overcome through other innovative developments in this area. It is clear that questions concerning appropriate techniques of assessment will provide a fruitful and valuable area for research for some time.

We have focused on these six research agenda issues because these seem to us to be significant and interesting. Clearly there are others. We have also presented these items singly, without indicating their interrelationships. Clearly there is scope for linked research on these separately identified issues.

References

Ahituv, N. and S. Neumann (1986), *Principles of Information Systems for Management*, W.C. Brown Publishers, Dubuque, Ia.

Andersen, E.S., K.V. Grude, T. Hang, and J.R. Turner (1988), *Goal Directed Project Management*, Kogan Page, London.

Argyris, C. (1988), 'Review essay: first- and second-order errors in managing strategic change: the role of organizational defensive routines', in A.M. Pettigrew (ed.), *The Management of Strategic Change*, Basil Blackwell, Oxford, pp. 342–51.

Ashridge Management Research (1988), *Management for the Future*, Ashridge Management Research Group/Foundation for Management Education, Berkhamsted.

Beckhard, R. and R. Harris (1977), *Organization Transitions: Managing complex change*, Addison Wesley, Reading, Mass.

Bennis, W.G. (1969), *Organization Development: Its nature, origins, and prospects*, Addison Wesley, Reading, Mass.

Birchall, D. (1975), *Job Design*, Gower, Aldershot.

Boddy, D. and D.A. Buchanan (1986), *The Management of New Technology*, Blackwell, Oxford.

Boddy, D. and D.A. Buchanan (1987), *The Technical Change Audit: Action for results*, Manpower Services Commission, Sheffield.

Boddy, D. and D.A. Buchanan (1992), *Take the Lead: Interpersonal skills for project managers*, Prentice Hall, Hemel Hempstead.

Bourgeois, L. and Brodwin, D. (1984), 'Strategic implementation: five approaches to an elusive phenomenon', *Strategic Management Journal*, vol. 5, pp. 241–64.

Boyatzis, R.E. (1982), *The Competent Manager: A model for effective performance*, John Wiley, New York.

British Telecom (1988), *Meeting Customer Requirements*, B.T., London.

Buchanan, D.A. (1979), *The Development of Job Design Theories and Techniques*, Saxon House, Aldershot.

Buchanan, D.A. (1991), 'Vulnerability and agenda: context and process in project management', *British Journal of Management*, vol. 2, no. 3, pp. 121–32.

Burns, T. (1961), 'Micropolitics: mechanisms of institutional change', *Administrative Science Quarterly*, vol. 5, pp. 257–81.

Burns, T. and G.M. Stalker (1961), *The Management of Innovation*, Tavistock, London.

Butler, R. (1991), *Designing Organizations: A decision-making perspective*, Routledge, London.

Carnall, C.A. (1990), *Managing Change in Organizations*, Prentice Hall, Hemel Hempstead.

Child, J. (1984), *Organization: A guide to problems and practice*, Harper & Row, London.

Coch, I. and J.R.P. French (1948), 'Overcoming resistance to change', *Human relations*, vol. 1, pp. 512–32.

Conway, B. and J. Powney (1990), *Assessment of Management Competences: Project report*, Employment Department (Training), London.

Coulson-Thomas, C.J. (1991), 'Developing tomorrow's professionals today', *Journal of European Industrial Training*, vol. 15, no. 1, pp. 3–11.

Coutts, S. (1989), 'When work is one big event after another', *The Sunday Times Scotland*, 19 February, p. 5.1.

Darnell, H. and M.W. Dale (1985), *Total Project Management: An integrated approach to the management of capital investment projects in industry*, British Institute of Management, London.

Devine, M. (1988), 'Flexibility's the aim for the global manager', *The Sunday Times*, 12 June, p. E22.

Dinsmore, P.C. (1990), *Human Factors in Project Management*, 2nd edn, American Management Association, New York.

Dopson, S. and R. Stewart (1990), 'What is happening to middle management?', *British Journal of Management*, vol. 1, no. 1, pp. 3–16.

Doz, Y.L. and C.K. Prahalad (1988), 'A process model of strategic redirection in large complex firms: the case of multinational corporations', in A.M. Pettigrew (ed.), *The Management of Strategic Change*, Basil Blackwell, Oxford, pp. 63–83.

Dunphy, D. (1981), *Organizational Change by Choice*, McGraw-Hill, Sydney.

Dutton, J.E. (1988), 'Understanding strategic agenda building and its implications for managing change', in Louis R. Pondy, Richard J. Boland Jr and Howard Thomas (eds), *Managing Ambiguity and Change*, John Wiley, Chichester, pp. 127–55.

Earl, M. and D. Skyrme (1990), 'Hybrid managers: what do we know about them?', *Oxford Institute of Information Management, Research and Discussion Papers*, Oxford, June.

Eason, K. (1988), *Informational Technology and Organizational Change*, Taylor Francis, London.

Eason, K. (1989), 'Designing systems to match organizational reality' in *People and Computers 5*, proceedings of the HCI '89 Conference, Nottingham, BCS/Cambridge University Press, pp. 57–69.

Emery, F.E. and E.L. Trist (1965), 'Causal texture of organizational environments', *Human Relations*, February, pp. 21–32.

Glaser, R. and M.T.H. Chi (1988), 'Overview', in Micheline T.H. Chi, Robert Glaser and Marshall J. Farr (eds), *The Nature of Expertise*, Lawrence Erlbaum, Hillsdale, NJ, pp. xv–xxviii.

Graham, R.J. (1985), *Project Management: Combining technical and behavioural approaches for effective implementation*, Van Nostrand Reinhold, New York.

Gunton, T. (1990), *Inside Information Technology: A practical guide to management issues*, Prentice Hall, New York.

Hamilton, S. (1988), 'The complex art of saying no', *Computing*, 13 October, pp. 30–1.

Handy, C. (1987), *The Making of Managers*, MSC/NEDO/BIM, London.

Harrison, F.L. (1985), *Advanced Project Management*, 2nd edn, Gower, Aldershot.

Hirschheim, R. (1985), *Office Automation: A Social and Organizational Perspective*, John Wiley, New York.

Huczynski, A.A. and D.A. Buchanan (1991), *Organizational Behaviour: An introductory text*, Prentice Hall, Hemel Hempstead.

Ingersoll Engineers (1987), *Technology in Manufacturing*, Rugby, Warwickshire.

Institute of Manpower Studies (1984), *Competence and Competition*, NEDO/MSC, London.

Ives, B. and M.H. Olson (1984), 'User involvement and MIS success: a review of research', *Management Science*, vol. 30, no. 5, pp. 586–603.

Johnson, E.J. (1988), 'Expertise and decision under uncertainty: performance and process', in Micheline T.H. Chi, Robert Glaser and Marshall J. Farr (eds), *The Nature of Expertise*, Lawrence Erlbaum, Hillsdale, NJ, pp. 209–28.

Johnson, G. (1990), 'Managing strategic change: the role of symbolic action', *British Journal of Management*, vol. 1, no. 4, pp. 183–200.

Kanter, R.M. (1983), *The Change Masters: Corporate entrepreneurs at work*, George Allen & Unwin, London.

Kanter, R.M. (1989), *When Giants Learn to Dance: Mastering the challenge of strategy, management and careers in the 1990s*, Simon & Schuster, London.

Kearney, A.T. (1990), *Barriers to the Successful Application of Information Technology*, Dept of Trade and Industry and CIMA, London.

Keen, P. (1981), 'Information systems and organizational change', in E. Rhodes and D. Weild (eds), *Implementing New Technologies: Choice, decision and change in manufacturing*, Basil Blackwell/The Open University Press, Oxford, pp. 361–73.

Kotter, J.P. and L.A. Schlesinger (1979), 'Choosing strategies for change', *Harvard Business Review*, vol. 57, no. 2, pp. 106–14.

Lawler, E.E. (1986), *High Involvement Management: Participative strategies for improving organizational performance*, Jossey-Bass, San Francisco.

Lesgold, A., H. Rubinson, P. Feltovich, R. Glaser, D. Klopfer, and Y. Wang, (1988), 'Expertise in a complex skill: diagnosing x-ray pictures', in Micheline T.H. Chi, Robert Glaser and Marshall J. Farr (eds), *The Nature of Expertise*, Lawrence Erlbaum, Hillsdale, NJ, pp. 311–42.

Long, R. (1987), *New Office Information Technology: Human and managerial implications*, Croom Helm, London.

McCaskey, M.B. (1988), 'The challenge of managing ambiguity and change', in Louis R. Pondy, Richard J. Boland Jr and Howard Thomas (eds), *Managing Ambiguity and Change*, John Wiley, Chichester, pp. 1–15.

McLoughlin, I. and J. Clark (1989), *Technological Change at Work*, The Open University Press, Milton Keynes.

Management Charter Initiative (1990), *Diploma Level Guidelines, National Forum for Management Education and Development*, report undated, London.

March, J.G. and J.P. Olson (1983), 'Organizing political life: what administrative reorganization tells us about government', *American Political Science Review*, vol. 77, no. 2, pp. 281–96.

Markus, M.L. (1983), 'Power, politics and MIS implementation', *Communications of the ACM*, vol. 26, no. 6, pp. 430–44.

Martin, C. (1988), *Computers and Senior Managers: Top management's response to interactive computing*, NCC Publications, Manchester.

Miles, R. (1990), 'A stitch in time', *Computing*, 11 October, pp. 22–3.

Mintzberg, H. (1989), *Mintzberg on Management: Inside our strange world of organizations*, Free Press/Macmillan, London.

Morley, L. (1990), 'How to convince the board with a hard sell', *Computing*, 29 November, pp. 20–21.

Morley, L. (1991), 'Expense account', *Computing*, 2 May, pp. 18–19.

Morris, P.W.G. and G.H. Hough (1987), *The Anatomy of Major Projects: A study of the reality of project management*, John Wiley, Chichester.

Mumford, E. (1981), 'Participative system design: structure and method', *Systems, Objectives, Solutions*, vol. 1, no. 1, pp. 5–19.

Mumford, E. and M. Weir (1979), *Computer Systems in Work Design – The ETHICS method*, Associated Business Press, London.

Obeng, E. (1990), 'Avoiding the fast-track pitfalls', *The Sunday Times*, 11 March, p. F1.

Palmer, C. and S. Ottley (1990), *From Potential to Reality: 'Hybrids' – a critical force in the application of information technology in the 1990s*, British Computer Society, London.

Peters, T. (1987), *Thriving on Chaos: Handbook for a managerial revolution*, Macmillan, London.

Pettigrew, A.M. (1985), *The Awakening Giant: Continuity and change in ICI*, Basil Blackwell, Oxford.

Pettigrew, A.M. (1987), 'Context and action in the transformation of the firm', *Journal of Management Studies*, vol. 24, no. 6, pp. 649–70.

Pettigrew, A.M. (1988), 'Introduction: researching strategic change', in A.M. Pettigrew, (ed.), *The Management of Strategic Change*, Basil Blackwell, Oxford, pp. 1–13.

Posner, M.I. (1988), 'What is it to be an expert?', in Micheline T.H. Chi, Robert Glaser and Marshall J. Farr (eds), *The Nature of Expertise*, Lawrence Erlbaum, Hillsdale, NJ, pp. xxix–xxxvi.

Preece, D.A. (1989), *Managing the Adoption of New Technology*, Routledge, London.

Quinn, J.B. (1980), *Strategies for Change: Logical incrementalism*, Richard D. Irwin, Homewood, Ill.

Quinn, J.B. (1982), 'Managing strategies incrementally', *Omega*, vol. 10, no. 6, pp. 613–27.

Quinn, R.E., S.R. Faerman, M.P. Thompson and M.R. McGrath (1990), *Becoming a Master Manager: A competency framework*, John Wiley, New York.

Ring, T. (1989), 'When it's not enough to be technically brilliant', *Computing*, 14 September, pp. 28–9.

Robey, D. and M. Lynne (1988), 'Rituals in information system design', in J.C. Wetherbe, V.T. Dock and S.L. Mandell (eds), *Readings in Information Systems: A managerial perspective*, West Publishing, St Paul, pp. 200–10.

Smith, S.D., C. Pell, P. Jones, M. Sloman and A. Blacknell (1989), *Management Challenge for the 1990s: The current education, training and development debate*, Training Agency, Sheffield.

Staszewski, J.J. (1988), 'Skilled memory and expert mental calculation', in Micheline T.H. Chi, Robert Glaser and Marshall J. Farr (eds), *The Nature of Expertise*, Lawrence Erlbaum, Hillsdale, NJ, pp. 71–128.

Thomson, A. (1991), 'Ten good things and ten bad things about MCI', British Academy of Management Newsletter, no. 11, September.

Toffler, A. (1970), *Future Shock*, Pan Books, London.

Towndrow, R. (1989), 'Training managers to live with change', *The Sunday Times*, 17 September, p. E1.

Training Commission (1988), *Classifying the Components of Management Competences*, Training Commission, Sheffield.

Voss, C.A. (1988), 'Implementation: a key issue in manufacturing technology: the need for a field of study', *Research Policy*, vol. 17, pp. 55–63.

Watson, G. (1966), *Resistance to Change*, National Training Laboratories, Washington, DC.

Whipp, R., R. Rosenfeld and A. Pettigrew (1988), 'Understanding strategic change processes: some preliminary British findings', in A. Pettigrew (ed.), *The Management of Strategic Change*, Blackwell, Oxford, pp. 14–55.

Recommended further reading

The recommendations that follow are aimed at students, particularly on masters' and diploma programmes in management, faced with assignment and project work, and thus looking for other sources of ideas, other empirical research, and for contrasting views and perspectives. Not all of the sources mentioned here have been used and cited in the text. We have, however, sought in this section to draw particular attention to a small number of particularly useful sources which we have already cited, while concentrating also on other items.

We have also indicated useful journals and magazines – most of which are obviously relevant and easily accessible, but which should not be overlooked as sources of information concerning current ideas, trends and research findings. It now takes considerable time to get books and academic articles into print, and recently generated thinking and findings of significance appear first in periodical sources.

The selection is inevitably biased in the direction of the sources that we have personally found helpful and interesting. We hope that you will find these sources useful too, and perhaps use these as pointers to other materials that you will no doubt find for yourself.

1 The state of the art

This chapter covered three areas – project management, participative management, and the politics of organizational change. The third theme is picked up again in more detail in Chapter 3, so we will concentrate here on the first two of those themes.

Readers interested in the management of new technology in particular may find interesting the authors' previous text which, although research based, sought to offer practical advice to IT managers with respect to organizational and implementation issues: Boddy, D. and Buchanan, D.A. (1986), *The Management of New Technology*, Basil Blackwell, Oxford. A recent wide-ranging review of research and other commentary on technology at work can be found in the following text, which is well informed, critical and has an accessible style: McLoughlin, I. and Clark, J. (1989), *Technological Change at Work*, Open University Press, Milton Keynes. One good conventional project management text is: Harrison, F.L. (1985), *Advanced Project Management*, 2nd edn, Gower, Aldershot.

The following provides unusually detailed insights into the management of large and publicly visible projects, such as the Channel Tunnel (1960–75), Concorde, the Advanced Passenger Train, the Thames barrier, and others. The authors develop their analysis to a detailed itemization of critical success factors on pages 265–6: Morris, P.W.G. and Hough, G.H. (1987), *The Anatomy of Major Projects: A study of the reality of project management*, John Wiley, Chichester.

We would also like to recommend two unconventional texts. The first offers a highly critical perspective on traditional project management and change implementation methods in management information systems environments – and both the criticisms and the new perspective on offer are interesting: Gunton, T. (1990), *Inside Information Technology: A practical guide to management issues*, Prentice Hall, Hemel Hempstead. The second offers a wealth of practical advice on specific change implementation techniques, from the conduct of planning meetings and special presentations, to the use of specific planning and problem-solving techniques such as force field analysis, and SWOT analysis, along with a large number of less familiar approaches and methods. This is an expensive publication, but is extremely useful to the harassed project manager looking for fresh and creative ideas to drive the change implementation process. The 'tool-kit' section is particularly helpful: Dawson, M. (1990), *Opportunities for Change*, Industrial Society Press, London.

The 'truth, trust, love and collaboration approach to change' has a long and consistent history, and finding sources in this area is not difficult. One interesting text which summarizes a range of management approaches, although from an American perspective, is: Lawler, E.E. (1986), *High Involvement Management: Participative strategies for improving organizational performance*, Jossey-Bass, San Francisco. We should also add that the publications of the American consultant Tom Peters also consistently reinforce the accepted participative wisdom. His work is too well publicized to need further citation here.

There are three journal publications that complement these sources. One is *The International Journal of Project Management*, which tends to publish technical articles with a conventional project management perspective – but does not publish articles in that style exclusively. A second, similar, publication is *Project Management Journal*. The third is *Computing*, the weekly journal of the British Computing Society, which regularly carries articles on project management, sometimes based on research, sometimes on current trends and on the experience of specific organizations.

2 Managing in quadrant four

The main classic source of the distinction between mechanistic and organic management systems repays reading today: Burns, T. and Stalker, G.M. (1961),

The Management of Innovation, Tavistock, London. Tom Burns and George Stalker worked in Scotland. A related research-based contribution with a similar argument about organizational integration and differentiation, from America, also highly influential, has been: Lawrence, P.R. and Lorsch, J.W. (1967), *Organization and Environment*, Harvard University Press, Boston, Mass.

An argument broadly similar to that of Burns and Stalker emerges nearly twenty years later, but with different terminology, whereby mechanistic becomes 'segmentalist' and organic becomes 'integrative'. This is in the interesting and once again influential work of Rosabeth Moss Kanter (1983), *The Change Masters: Corporate entrepreneurs at work*, George Allen & Unwin, London. Kanter is among the few commentators on change management to recognize the significance of what she calls 'power skills', and of the manipulative dimension of the work of the change agent in forming coalitions, in constructing the change implementation process ('change architect skills'), in blocking resistance, and in choosing carefully the language in which change proposals are couched. Her more recent work on the relationship between structure and environment is also of interest, although written in a different, typically American managerialist, style: Kanter, R.M. (1989), *When Giants Learn to Dance: Mastering the challenge of strategy, management and careers in the 1990s*, Simon & Schuster, London.

Another writer, consultant and researcher who recognizes the same pressures on the change agent is Peter Keen. The article cited in the text has been reprinted in a more accessible source, which contains other articles on change management with respect to manufacturing technology: Keen, P. (1981), 'Information systems and organizational change', in E. Rhodes and D. Weild (eds), *Implementing New Technologies: Choice, decision and change in manufacturing*, Basil Blackwell/ Open University Press, Oxford, pp. 361–73.

A shortened and more focused account of the research reported in Chapter 2 can be found in: Buchanan, D.A. (1991), 'Vulnerability and agenda: context and process in project management', *British Journal of Management*, vol. 2, no. 3, pp. 121–32. The *British Journal of Management* is a relatively recent arrival on the British academic management stage, and is into its second volume at the time of writing. It has already published a number of articles relevant to the themes of this text, and can be expected to be a useful source of such material in the future. The reader seeking information on other current environmental influences on management and organization structure can frequently find relevant items in *The Economist*, *The Financial Times*, *The Sunday Times*, and *Management Today* (the magazine of the British Institute of Management).

---

3   Models of process

The key sources for this chapter are from Andrew M. Pettigrew: (1973) *The Politics of Organizational Decision-Making*, Tavistock, London; (1985) *The Awakening Giant:*

Continuity and change in ICI, Basil Blackwell, Oxford; 'Context and action in the transformation of the firm', *Journal of Management Studies* (1987), vol. 24, no. 6, pp. 649–70; and as editor, *The Management of Strategic Change* (1988), Basil Blackwell, Oxford. Pettigrew's work has been highly influential, and *The Awakening Giant* in particular has been widely cited. We have been highly selective in extracting from that book which also offers detailed and fascinating insights into change and organizational development in a major corporation. Pettigrew's style may frustrate the practising manager in a hurry to find practical advice, but the theoretical developments and research agenda are highly significant. Readers looking for a summary of the overall argument should turn first to the 1987 article.

The following source has also been influential and widely cited, in arguing for the blend of rational and political in organizational change: Quinn, J.B. (1980), *Strategies for Change: Logical incrementalism*, Irwin, Homewood, Ill.

Pettigrew and Quinn are not the easiest authors to read. A gentler introduction to contemporary thinking can be found in the work of Colin Carnall, who has a short chapter on 'managing corporate politics' supporting the arguments developed in this book: Carnall, C.A. (1990), *Managing Change in Organizations*, Prentice Hall, Hemel Hempstead. Carnall also offers some interesting case studies and diagnostic frameworks that can be used in management development settings.

Texts that deal with the negotiating and influencing skills of management, and which are of direct interest to the change agent, are plentiful. Here are two examples: Bell, C.R. (1982), *Influencing: Marketing the ideas that matter*, Learning Concepts, Austin, Tex.; and Scott, B. (1988), *Negotiating: Constructive and competitive negotiations*, Paradigm Publishing, London. A more comprehensive, and more theoretically rich, treatment of the interpersonal and diagnostic skills of management can be found in: Wright, P.L. and Taylor, D.S. (1984), *Improving Leadership Performance*, Prentice Hall, Hemel Hempstead.

The *Journal of Management Studies* and *Organization Studies* are useful sources of further articles dealing with the issues raised in this chapter.

---

4   A model of expertise

The management competence debate in Britain has generated a large and growing literature, and it is not entirely clear at the time of writing how the Management Charter Initiative will develop. The work which triggered this movement was: Boyatzis, R.E. (1982), *The Competent Manager: A model for effective performance*, John Wiley, New York.

Two useful sources dealing with the general issues and with company specific approaches are: Jacobs, R. (1989), 'Getting the measure of management competence', *Personnel Management*, June, pp. 32–7; and Jacobs, R. (1989),

'Cadbury's dictionary of competence', *Personnel Management*, July, pp. 44–8. Cadbury is not the only company to develop an in-house approach to these issues. Jacobs in the first of these two articles also identifies the competences which W.H. Smith is seeking in their recruitment of graduates.

The Management Charter Initiative has published its own sets of guidelines to the national standards at certificate and diploma levels, and will no doubt produce a standard for masters' level programmes at some point. The emphasis in this approach is on assessment of competence through performance in a management role, not on the delivery of understanding through lectures which are assessed through examinations and essays. This emphasis has led to some innovative work with respect to how competence can actually be assessed in other more practical (but potentially more expensive and time-consuming) ways. The elements of the emerging assessment approach are best summarized in: Conway, B. and Powney, J. (1990), *Assessment of Management Competences: Project report*, The Employment Department (Training), London.

Another American perspective, from two well-known authors, on these issues is also of value. The following text identifies (p. 23) a list of eighty-four skills for 'the organizational development practitioner' (i.e. change agent), including fifty core skills and thirty-four advanced skills that the more mature practitioner is also expected to possess. This is a typical, wide-ranging American text with many useful theoretical frameworks and case studies: Cummings, T.G. and Huse, E.F. (1989), *Organization Development and Change*, 4th edn, West Publishing Company, St Paul.

The Institute of Personnel Management has a clear interest in developments in this area, and their monthly journal *Personnel Management* is a useful source of up-to-date materials – theoretical and with respect to company practice and experience. The new academic publication, *Human Resource Management Journal*, is also an authoritative source of materials in this area.

The companion text to this volume offers a slightly different perspective on the competences of the change agent, and is directed primarily at the development and application of specific practical skills, avoiding the extended references to theoretical accounts provided here: Boddy, D. and Buchanan, D.A. (1992), *Take the Lead: Interpersonal skills for project managers*, Prentice Hall, Hemel Hempstead.

---

5 Management development strategies

Readers looking for a brief history of management development in Britain, including the Management Charter Initiative, an account of methods, an exploration of future needs, and an argument in support of a systematic approach should turn to: Sadler, P. (1989), 'Management development', in Keith Sisson (ed.), *Personnel Management in Britain*, Basil Blackwell, Oxford, pp. 222–46.

Action learning as a management development approach has a long history, and Sadler introduces this in his chapter. The original version can be found in two publications by R.W. Revans: *Developing Effective Managers* (1971), Longmans, London; and 'Action learning projects', in B. Taylor and G. Lippit (eds), *Management Development and Training Handbook* (1975), McGraw Hill, London.

One of the sources cited in the text provides a readable summary of the main influential reports and other publications in Britain in the 1980s which conditioned the management development debate and triggered the Management Charter Initiative: Smith, S.D., Pell, C., Jones, P., Sloman, M. and Blacknell, A. (1989), *Management Challenge for the 1990s: The current education, training and development debate*, Training Agency, Sheffield.

The journals *Personnel Review* and *Journal of European Industrial Training* regularly offer other articles, usually with an eye towards management practice in addition to theoretical developments. Two articles from the former are particularly helfpul in documenting the contemporary state of thinking in the management development field: Storey, J. (1989), 'Management development: a literature review, part one', *Personnel Review*, vol. 18, no. 4, pp. 3–18; Storey, J. (1989), 'Management development: a literature review, part two', *Personnel Review*, vol. 18, no. 5, pp. 3–11.

Index